P9-CKU-496

Nationalism in Europe

CAMBRIDGE PERSPECTIVES IN HISTORY
Series editors: Richard Brown and David Smith

Nationalism in Europe, 1789–1945

Timothy Baycroft

Lecturer in History,
University of Sheffield

CAMBRIDGE
UNIVERSITY PRESS

CAMBRIDGE UNIVERSITY PRESS
Cambridge, New York, Melbourne, Madrid, Cape Town, Singapore, São Paulo

Cambridge University Press
The Edinburgh Building, Cambridge CB2 2RU, UK

www.cambridge.org
Information on this title: www.cambridge.org/9780521598712

© Cambridge University Press 1998

This book is in copyright. Subject to statutory exception
and to the provisions of relevant collective licensing agreements,
no reproduction of any part may take place without
the written permission of Cambridge University Press.

First published 1998
5th printing 2005

Printed in the United Kingdom at the University Press, Cambridge

A catalogue record for this publication is available from the British Library

ISBN-13 978-0-521-59871-2 paperback
ISBN-10 0-521-59871-0 paperback

ACKNOWLEDGEMENTS
Cover, Musée de la Ville de Paris/Musée du Petit-Palais/Bridgeman Art Library;
15, Prado, Madrid/Index/Bridgeman Art Library, London/New York; 20, Louvre,
Paris/Peter Willi/Bridgeman Art Library, London/New York; 27, Musée des
Beaux-Arts, Lille/Giraudon/Bridgeman Art Library, London/New York;
72, Imperial War Museum; 80, David King Collection.

The cover illustration by Félix Philippoteaux (c. 1815–84) shows the French
poet and statesman Alphonse de Lamartine (1790–1869) rejecting the red
flag in 1848.

Contents

Contents

Introduction

In recent years, nationalism in Europe has been a topic attracting increasing attention from both scholars and the general public. The contribution of this book is not to add a new dimension to all of the work which has come before, but to provide an overview in order to introduce the reader to the most important themes and debates. It does not attempt to provide an explanation and chronology of the rise of each and every nationalist movement in Europe, but instead aims to come to grips with the underlying causes of the growth of modern European nationalism as a doctrine, and to understand its historical significance and its consequences for the development of European politics and society over slightly more than a century and a half. The question of the roots of nationalism prior to 1789 is also not explored. This does not imply that no such roots exist; it seems more important to underline the novelty of the specifically modern character of nationalism after the French Revolution.

The first chapter, after an explanation of the terms 'nation', 'nationalism' and 'nationalist movement', sets out to explain how these terms came to acquire their modern meanings around the time of the French Revolution, and how they initially spread through Europe in the wake of Napoleon's armies. Chapter 2 traces the development of nationalism from its rejection by the European powers after the fall of Napoleon up to the unification of Germany and the general acceptance of the idea of the nation. Chapters 3 and 4 examine the theory of the nation in more detail, looking at different ways of defining the nation in the nineteenth century and the possible combinations of elements used to construct national mythologies, as well as the processes by which they are created. Chapter 5 examines the criticism of nationalism and nationalist theory and the historical interpretation of the nation-states advanced by Karl Marx and his followers. Rather than a nation-based theory, they put forward a class theory that challenged national loyalties and called instead for international worker solidarity. Chapter 6 deals with the popular phase of nationalism, from 1870 to the First World War, and describes the passage of nationalism and national identity from the elite to the masses of Europe. In Chapter 7, the role of national competition in European expansion through imperialism is explored, along with the contributions of extra-European empires to the development of national identities within Europe. Chapter 8 takes us from the First World War to the Second, through the phase of greatest acceptance of the idea of the nation for the organisation of European society, and examines the conflicts which resulted from it.

1

Each chapter is followed by one or more related primary documents, which will provide the reader with contemporary views, analysis and in some cases nationalist expression and opinions in order to supplement and illustrate the themes discussed. The book contains a bibliographic guide indicating some of the major works about nationalism, and it ends with a chronology of a selection of the major events relating to nationalism in the period.

The French Revolution and the idea of the nation

The emergence of nations or nation-states is arguably the most influential development in Europe during the nineteenth century. The accompanying ideology of nationalism was associated with various aspects of democratic and social progress, and lay at the root of many of the major conflicts of the century, culminating in the First World War. Almost all of the major European intellectuals, politicians, reformers and activists were at some point in their careers caught up in the debates about nationalist ideas and policies. It could even be said that the history of Europe from 1789 to 1945 is synonymous with the history of the growth and development of modern nations.

Characteristics of the modern idea of the nation

What is it that made the idea of the nation so powerful, and what special qualities do nations possess that give them such tremendous influence? Nations have several features that distinguish them from other forms of social organisation. A nation is a group of people identified as sharing any number of real or perceived characteristics – such as common ancestry, language, religion, culture, historical traditions and shared territory – the members of which can identify themselves and the others as belonging to the group, and who have the will or desire to remain as a group, united through some form of organisation, most often political.

Not every nation has the same combination of characteristics to define it; some emphasise one type of common feature, while others define themselves principally by another. France is defined by territory and language, Belgium by religion, Germany by common ancestry. Nor do all nations need to have all of these characteristics in common; in some cases a nation may demonstrate some elements of diversity. Switzerland may have four languages, but it is still considered to be a nation on account of its common republican historical tradition and its geographical coherence.

It is essential that the individual members are aware of the ties that link them together as a nation or a national community. The mutual awareness and affirmation of these ties, and identification with other members, is what gives individuals their national identity and generates the will to form a nation in the first instance, and then to hold it together. Without the will or desire on the part of the people to remain a nation, some shared characteristics are not sufficient to form a nation. For example, Austria and Germany share a common language, but do not form parts of the same nation because the respective populations do not consider themselves associated with each other and do not have sufficient desire to be considered as one nation. In other words, they have different identities. The strength of national identity and the sense of belonging increases as people become conscious of the characteristics they have in common with the other members of their nation.

Beyond shared characteristics and a national identity, nations also need to be actively preserved and supported by some form of political structure or organisation. The classic and simplest of these structures is the nation-state, where the representatives of the nation run the government and the state apparatus, and the state boundaries coincide with those of the nation. It is possible, however, for nations and national identity to be supported by a political structure of opposition, seeking power within a state or through political division, although the goal for the nationalists is always to attain nation-state status.

Once individuals feel that they belong to a nation, can identify their nation and its characteristics and clearly define its membership, a possibility for nationalism and nationalist movements is opened up. Nationalism is a belief that the shared characteristics of the nation are valuable and need to be preserved, and that in order to achieve that the national community has a legitimate right to form a separate political state, independent from other perceived nations, in which the nation or the people are sovereign. Nationalism is more than patriotism, which is a sentiment of loyalty to the nation to which one belongs, because it includes the beliefs that one's own nation has a higher calling and greater value than other nations, and that the nation is the only legitimate source of power. Nationalism supports the belief that perceived threats or enemies to the nation need to be eliminated, destroyed or defeated – be they internal oppressors, agents of foreign domination or merely other, rival nations – in order to raise the worldly status or rank and increase the glory and the prestige of the nation.

Once feelings of nationalism are widespread, they can give rise to nationalist movements. A nationalist movement is a politically active group seeking to give this kind of power or independence, which is necessary for the preservation of the nation, to the nation as they define it. This may be through separation from a larger state considered to be oppressing the nation through external political control, or through the unification of what were formerly separate states but which collectively form only one nation. With these types of national movement, the goal is to make the political boundaries of the state coincide with the boundaries of the nation or, in other words, to provide a durable political structure which will be able to defend the nation.

Not all national movements seek to change the boundaries of states. Often the goal of the national movement is simply to put the ultimate political power into the hands of 'the nation' or its representatives, and to take it away from some kind of oppressive ruler, be it a monarch, emperor or dictator. This kind of nationalism has to do with sovereignty. It is the people, the whole population, that makes up the nation, from the upper classes down to the lowliest, humblest peasant and worker. The people or the nation is held to be the only true source of political power, and the divine right of kings and the right of the strongest to impose their will on others is denied. The only power that can be considered legitimate is that which comes from the nation as a whole. Nationalist doctrine is therefore linked to democracy, for no one ruler should have the right to have power over the nation, which should be able to determine its own future and set its own rules.

The nation and nationalism as we have defined them, combining the belief in the sovereignty of the people with an emotional attachment to the nation, are essentially modern notions, and have only recently come to play a significant role in European affairs in this form. The remainder of this chapter will be devoted to an examination of the origins of the idea of the nation and nationalism as significant forces during the last two centuries, and of the specific character-istics that made them so powerful.

The French Revolution

The dawning of the age of the modern nation came at the end of the eighteenth century in France in the form of the French Revolution. Beginning in 1789, the revolutionaries sought to free the French people from what they considered the tyranny of the French monarchy during the *ancien régime*, embodied in its king, Louis XVI. The absolute power of the Bourbon kings had to be brought to an end, and replaced with the more legitimate authority of the nation – as summed up in the motto of the French Revolution: *Liberté, égalité, fraternité*.

Law and the nation

The roots of the revolutionary idea of the nation can be found in the philosophy of natural law developed during the Enlightenment. This philosophy was opposed to the traditional idea of divine law according to which all political authority and legitimacy ultimately belongs to God, as expressed by his representatives, the king and the church. For the Enlightenment thinkers who favoured natural law, such as Jean-Jacques Rousseau, sovereignty is not supra-natural but belongs solely with the people. To explain how people can exercise this sovereignty, these writers developed theories of the Social Contract, whereby certain groups form nations which choose their rulers from among themselves. Each individual has a partial say in the rules, and because of that part agrees to obey them.

The revolutionaries of 1789 were the first in Europe to put this notion of the nation into practice in legal and political terms, and to use it as the primary basis for the legal system of government. The nation was for them the only legitimate source of power, which could be exercised only in the name of, and for the greater good of, the nation as a whole. In this way the nation became not merely one among several forces competing for political control, but the *only* legitimate source of power – it was the foundation and the root source of all authority. With these reasons they justified the overthrow of the absolute monarchy based on divine law, and tried to set up a regime which would place the power where it legitimately belonged: with the French people.

The process began when Louis XVI, because of financial difficulties, was forced to call a meeting of the Estates-General on 5 May 1789. The Estates-General consisted of three parts: the First Estate, comprising the nobility; the Second Estate, made up of the clergy; and the Third Estate, representing everyone else. Traditionally, each estate met separately and had one vote, so that although the Third Estate represented 96 per cent of the population, it only had one vote out of three. Almost immediately, reforms to the system were put forward by the members of the Third Estate, who called themselves nationals and patriots. They were joined by some of the lower clergy and a few enlightened nobles such as the marquis de Lafayette. They wanted to double the number of representatives of the Third Estate, to have the three estates meet together in one forum and to change the voting system so that each representative had one vote, altering the balance of decision-making power.

These national and patriot reformers were inspired by a book by the abbé Emmanuel Joseph Sieyès entitled *What is the Third Estate?* He defined the Third Estate as the whole of the nation, asserting that all members of the nation were citizens, and equal before the law (see Document 1.1). Sieyès rejected the principle of class and special upper-class feudal privileges, and claimed that the first two estates did not even qualify as parts of the nation. In his work, the idea of the legitimacy of the nation emerges at the same time as and in close association with the idea of the equality of all citizens.

This assertive group gradually gained power, and their demands were met; on 9 July 1789 the three estates met together under the new title of the National Constituent Assembly, with the established principle of voting by head, not by estate. Their first task was to draw up a constitution for France. The result of their deliberations was a constitutional monarchy based upon the principle of national sovereignty represented by the members of the assembly, and an accompanying document called the Declaration of the Rights of Man and the Citizen, accepted by the assembly on 26 August 1789 and proclaimed on 14 September 1789 (see Document 1.2). It affirmed the principle of equal rights for all individuals and the inviolable right of all nations to determine their own fate.

The constitution and the Declaration of the Rights of Man and the Citizen marked the accomplishment of the first phase of the revolution from the point of view of the development of nationalism, the legal phase. At this point laws were put in place and principles firmly established to ensure that the nation was the source of all legitimacy and hence all legality, and that all citizens were equal before the law and had inalienable individual rights as citizens. This marked the fulfilment of the ideals of the Enlightenment and set a precedent for the development of modern legal systems. The fact that the declaration was the first major accomplishment of the revolutionary National Constituent Assembly demonstrates how central this legal concept of the nation was in the collective vision of what the revolution was to accomplish and how preoccupied the revolutionaries were with it.

Emotional nationalism and the revolutionary wars

The second major element of modern nations and nationalism to come out of the French Revolution was the forging of a strong emotional link by the people to their nation. The growth and development of these strong personal ties with the nation came about through the conflicts between revolutionary France and other European powers. Numerous aristocrats had fled France in the face of the revolution, and they petitioned foreign rulers to attack France in order to re-establish the absolute monarchy and feudal rights. Many of the revolutionary leaders were no less eager to enter into conflict with foreign rulers in order to bring the principles of equality and citizenship to the other oppressed peoples of Europe. Evidence of this sentiment can be seen in a speech given by Maximilien Robespierre in 1793 (see Document 1.3), in which he asserts that the principle of freedom for nations can and should be extended beyond the borders of France and applied to all peoples. France was thought to be a kind of liberator for all oppressed peoples and nations.

The key motivating force behind the revolutionary wars was nationalism, and a wave of patriotic rhetoric accompanied the growth of support for the wars. The revolutionary leaders gave patriotic speeches such as Georges Danton's famous call to defend the nation, claiming that to defeat one's enemies required daring, more daring and always daring. They saw the foreign enemies as traitors to the nation, and clamoured for war to defeat the enemies of liberty once and for all. With these wars and the development of the mass army the image of the 'nation at arms' was born. It was in this period of war that the soldiers began to compose and to sing patriotic songs for motivation. The *Marseillaise*, which has become France's national anthem, was composed as a war song to motivate soldiers and generate enthusiasm for the revolutionary wars.

The first of the major revolutionary wars began in 1792 and was against Austria, whose emperor, Leopold, was Marie-Antoinette's brother. He was soon joined in the conflict by his ally, Prussia. After some early defeats, the French began to rally their army. No longer merely a professional group of paid soldiers doing their job, the French army grew and transformed itself into a truly national army, motivated by patriotism and the defence of its homeland. Encouraged by patriotic sentiment, French citizens engaged to fight for the freedom they had won through the revolution. The turning point came on 20 September 1792 at the battle of Valmy, where the French forces, shouting *Vive la nation!*, defeated the Prussians. With that and subsequent victories came the celebration and further glorification of the nation. Johann Wolfgang von Goethe – the German poet – was present at the battle, and wrote that he was witness to the dawning of a new era in world history.

The patriotic fervour leading to the revolutionary wars, and the willingness of the citizens to fight for their nation, emerged from what may be seen as the second phase of the revolution, the emotional phase. The nation became more than simply a foundation for a legal system based upon the principle of equality of citizens before the law; it also became something possessing numerous praiseworthy qualities, to be valued for its own sake and worth fighting and dying for. Individuals developed emotional attachments to their nation that went beyond a belief in the values of the Enlightenment. The revolutionary and later the Napoleonic mass army of volunteers and conscripts served as a kind of melting pot in which national sentiment was first taught to the French people.

Although the general trend was clearly towards increased patriotism, it would be excessive to claim that the French people's newly discovered emotional attachment to the nation developed entirely without opposition. The uprising of civil war in the west of France in the Vendée (which remained faithful to the king and the Roman Catholic church) demonstrates that right from the beginning the attempt to create French national unity provoked a certain level of internal violence and tension.

Thus the idea of the nation which emerged from the French Revolution had a legal and an emotional dimension. The legal side had its origins in Enlightenment thinking about natural justice, and asserted the principles of equality of all individuals as a part of the nation and of the nation as the sovereign authority upon which the legal and political system should be based. It implied a fundamental reorganisation of the state and its laws so that the feudal system was completely dismantled and the privileges of the nobility were eliminated. The emotional tie to the nation and the idea of the nation grew in the face of internal and external threats, which enabled individual members to identify personally with the nation, and to become sentimentally attached to it in such a way as to be willing to fight for its preservation and glory. The combination of the two dimensions helped to contribute to the tremendous appeal of the idea of the nation, and is a partial explanation of why nations and nationalism came to be so important a force in nineteenth- and twentieth-century Europe. The emotions that nationalism can generate add considerable weight and enthusiasm to the purely legal, intellectual arguments.

Throughout the French Revolution and the revolutionary wars, this complex idea of the nation became a powerful political reality, both at a legal level within France and through the ideological and military conflicts it provoked throughout Europe. The reality of the wars forced large segments of European society to think about the ideological conflict that lay at their root. Not only did nationalism grow and take hold within France, but the seeds of future nationalism were also sown in the countries that came into contact with revolutionary and Napoleonic France.

This particular idea of the nation and this form of nationalism did not exist prior to the French Revolution. The nation as both a legal *and* an emotional principle accompanied by a powerful, popular political force called nationalism is what characterises the modern period of history. It was in France during the revolution that the nation appeared in its modern form, and the following century and a half would see Europe transformed by the influence and development of nation-states, becoming permeated with nationalism and its effects. The changes were not straightforward and uniform, however, and the idea of the nation underwent numerous transformations as it spread through

Europe, adapting to local conditions. The variety of characteristics used to define nations and the different political conditions in which nationalist debates took place determined both the manner in which each nation conceived itself and the ways in which nationalism influenced its growth and development.

Revolutionary ideas of the nation

1.1 Excerpt from Emmanuel Sieyès, *What is the Third Estate?*

Who then would dare to say that the Third Estate does not have in it everything necessary to form a complete nation? . . .

What is a nation? A body of associates living under a *common* law and represented in the same *legislature*.

Is it not too certain that the noble class has privileges, exemptions, and even rights separate from the rights of the large body of citizens? Through these they are not a part of the common order; of the common law. Hence, their civil rights make of them a separate people in the grand nation . . .

With respect to their *political* rights, they exercise them separately as well. They have their own representatives, who are in no way charged with the authority of the people. The body of their deputies sits apart, and when assembled in the same hall as the deputies of the simple citizens, it is not less true that its representation is distinct and separate: it is foreign to the nation in principle, since its mission does not come from the people, and in object, which consists of defending, not the general interests, but their specific interests.

The Third [Estate] therefore comprises everything which belongs to the nation; and everything which is not the Third cannot consider itself as being a part of the nation. What is the Third? Everything.

. . .

I request that we pay attention to the enormous difference between the assembly of the Third Estate and those of the other two orders. The first represents 25 million men and deliberates the interests of the nation. The two others, even if called to meet, have only the power of around two hundred thousand individuals, and think only of their privileges. The Third [Estate] on its own, we are told, cannot form the Estates-General. Well! So much the better! It will make up the *National Assembly* . . . I say that the deputies of the clergy and the nobility have nothing in common with the national representation, and no alliance is possible between the three orders of the Estates-General.

Source: E. J. Sièyes, *Qu'est-ce que le Tiers Etat?*, Paris, 1982 (originally published January 1789); trans. T. Baycroft

1.2 Excerpt from the Declaration of the Rights of Man and the Citizen, August 1789

Preamble

The representatives of the French people, meeting as the National Assembly, believing that the ignorance, forgetting and contempt of the rights of man are the only causes of public misfortune and of the corruption of governments, have resolved to set out in a solemn declaration the natural, inalienable and sacred rights of man, so that this declaration, constantly present for all the members of the social body, will remind them continually of their rights and their duties . . .

I. Men are born and remain free and equal in rights. Social distinctions can only be founded upon common utility.

. . .

III. The principle of all sovereignty lies fundamentally with the nation; no body, no individual can exercise authority which does not expressly emanate from it.

. . .

VI. The law is the expression of the general will; all citizens have the right to work towards its formation, personally or through their representatives; it must be the same for all, whether in protecting or punishing.

Source: Trans. T. Baycroft

1.3 Excerpt from the 'On property' speech by Maximilien Robespierre, 24 April 1793

The Committee has again completely forgotten to consecrate the responsibilities of fraternity which link all men to all nations, and their right to mutual assistance. It seems to have ignored the basis of the eternal alliance between peoples against tyrants. One would think that your declaration was made for a herd of human creatures parked in a distant corner of the globe, and not for the immense family to which nature has given the earth as its domain.

I propose to fill this large gap with the following articles. They cannot but win for you the esteem of the world's peoples; it is true that they may have the disadvantage of pitting you against the kings without the opportunity to turn back. I admit that this inconvenience does not frighten me; it will not ever frighten those who do not in their hearts want merely to reconcile themselves with these kings. Here are my four articles:

I. Men of all countries are brothers, and the different peoples must help each other as much as their power allows as if they were citizens of the same state.

II. Whoever oppresses one nation declares himself the enemy of all nations.

III. Those who wage war against a people to stop the progress of liberty and to negate the rights of man must be pursued by all, not as ordinary enemies, but as assassins, brigands and rebels.

IV. Kings, aristocrats, tyrants, whoever they may be, are slaves revolting against the sovereign of the earth, which is the human species, and against the legislator of the universe, which is nature.

Source: H. Morse Stephens (ed.), *The principal speeches of the statesmen and orators of the French Revolution 1789–1795*, vol. II, Oxford, 1892, pp. 366–70; trans. T. Baycroft

Document case-study questions

1 Why does the Third Estate alone represent the nation, according to Document 1.1?

2 How did the interpretation of the nation in Document 1.1 influence the development of the French Revolution?

3 How does Document 1.2 reflect the legal interpretation of the nation?

4 What are the political consequences of the sentiments expressed in Document 1.3?

5 Compare and contrast the sentiments expressed in Documents 1.1–1.3.

The growth of a Europe of nations, 1814–1870

The treaty of Vienna in 1815 marked the defeat of Napoleon and the end of French influence and domination in Europe. It was a triumph for the traditional monarchies; the Bourbon king was restored to his throne in France, and the victors sought to re-establish the pre-revolutionary order across Europe. While several of the countries retained constitutions, this victory nevertheless implied the abandonment of the nation as the legal principle for the foundation of states, and the return of absolutism to most of Europe. Territory was redistributed in accordance with the balance of power among the major monarchs, without regard to nationality in any form. Russia dominated eastern Europe, Austria held the German and Italian states under its wing and Great Britain ruled the seas. Prussia and France were strong enough to prevent either one of the two big continental powers from taking over.

It seemed that nothing was left of the influence of the revolution, and that support for revolutionary principles had disappeared for good. One essential element remained, however, and that was the idea of the nation. In spite of the treaty of Vienna, and the apparent victory for absolutism and the traditional order of the eighteenth century, the new concept of nations and nationality had spread throughout Europe and would resurface so as to transform the face of European society and politics gradually. In order to see how this was accomplished, we shall first examine the nature of Napoleonic Europe to understand how the idea was exported from France.

The Napoleonic wars and the rise of nationalism

While revolutionary France had only a limited impact on the rest of Europe, France under Napoleon came to dominate the continent. Napoleon had a great plan for Europe, in part motivated by his quest for greater personal power and influence, and in part by a desire to see the social and administrative organisation he had put into place in France extended to the other countries. Through the Civil or Napoleonic Code, he hoped to create a new European civilisation which would be based on the principles of 1789 as he saw them. By this, Napoleon thought mainly of the suppression of feudalism, and of secularism and the equality of all before the law. Although he secured a large nationalist, patriotic following in France, by declaring himself emperor he had abandoned the legal principle of the nation as the sovereign basis for the state and the law as it had been conceived by the early leaders of the revolution.

In spite of Napoleon's objectives for his greater European empire, it was not his social and administrative organisation that he left behind in Europe, but the seeds of nationalist sentiments which would determine the course of European history for more than one hundred years. Based upon resentment of French influence and domination, several other European countries developed emotional, nationalist responses.

Great Britain not only lived through 22 years of almost uninterrupted war with France, but after 1807 had to deal with the continental blockade imposed by Napoleon. This blockade led to a crisis of overproduction with significant consequences for the British economy. The resulting hardship and suffering, combined with the threat of invasion and the leading role of the British among the anti-Napoleonic armies after the battle of Trafalgar, contributed to increasing the British national sentiment that had already begun to form among the commercial and political elites who were central to the country's economic greatness.

In the Netherlands, the Dutch traders had not only suffered from the continental blockade of Great Britain, but were also excluded from French and southern European markets by trade barriers put into place by Napoleon. They looked back at the Dutch greatness of the sixteenth and seventeenth centuries, and their nationalist resentment of the French led them to revolt against Napoleon in 1813.

In Italy, where Napoleon had brought greater unity among the different Italian states and revived the use of the term 'Italy', the people began to resent the economic hardships brought about by the blockade, the large numbers of their soldiers killed fighting for Napoleon, and the number of Italian artistic treasures which had been taken away to Paris. Some Italian poets began to call for Italian unity and independence, and they were soon followed by other members of the Italian intellectual and military elite.

In the German states, it was the collapse of Prussia at the battle of Jena in 1806 and the harshness of the subsequent French domination that pushed German intellectuals such as Johann Gottlieb Fichte (see Document 2.1) and Karl von Stein to call for unity and support from the greater German nation, which was politically divided but culturally uniform. From that time forward, German political unification and liberalisation was a major preoccupation of the German intellectual elite.

These nationalist reactions to Napoleonic domination were by no means felt by the majority of the population in the occupied countries, but the minority who voiced them were persistent enough not to disappear completely from the scene after Napoleon's fall in 1814–15 and the return to the pre-revolutionary political structure. The years that followed the treaty of Vienna in 1815 would see the steady growth and development of these nationalist sentiments, differing slightly in emphasis and form depending upon the country in question. The active minority who embraced nationalism sought to increase nationalist feeling and win support for the nationalist movements which were already forming around Europe.

The nationalist elite

Who was it, then, who found nationalism appealing, and what did they stand to gain from the development of nationalism in Europe in the early nineteenth century? For the most part it was the small landowners – occasionally even the lower nobility – as well as the growing middle class and lower middle class. Constrained and discontented within the Europe of monarchy and empire, the small landholders hoped to increase their standing through national movements. The middle class of professionals, administrators and intellectuals also sought an avenue for advancement and a means to penetrate the closed elite of aristocratic society.

A crucial defining feature of those who were attracted to nationalist ideals was education. It was the educated classes as a whole, rather than the bourgeois business elite, that kept nationalism alive in the decades following the fall of Napoleon. In his *Addresses to the German nation*, delivered in 1807–08, Fichte made it quite clear that the leadership of the national struggle needed to be assumed by what he called the educated classes – by which he implied the former students, professionals, middle and senior bureaucrats, artists and intellectuals who attended his university lectures and read his books (see Document 2.1). Business leaders were often as interested in developing international markets and maintaining European trading links as they were in setting up restrictive national economic territories, and were therefore cautious with respect to nationalism at this early stage.

With a very small elite it was possible to continue using Latin and French as international languages of the educated, but as more people received secondary school education, the numbers seeking administrative advancement rose and it became increasingly desirable to begin to use 'national' languages. Starting in the early nineteenth century, the demand for written works and communication in German, Czech, Romanian, Polish, Dutch and other – soon to be labelled 'national' – languages began to increase.

This emphasis on 'national' languages was especially marked among the peoples of central and eastern Europe. The Hungarian Academy was created in 1825 and sought to encourage a renewal of the use of Hungarian; it was followed in 1834 by the publication of the first Hungarian-language newspaper, the *Pest Hirlap*. In Russia, writers such as Aleksander Pushkin began to encourage the Russian elite to abandon French in favour of Russian. Thus language became an important element in thinking about and defining nations as nationalism spread outwards from France through Europe.

The emotional, sentimental nationalist reaction to Napoleon's political domination first brought nationalism to the rest of Europe, but the doctrine of political equality and liberty appealed strongly to the rising educated classes and stimulated much of the nationalist intellectual writing and agitation that appeared. The intellectuals stood to benefit more than others from the kind of political equality championed during the French Revolution, and from the adoption of their own languages. The dominant artistic and intellectual movement of the early nineteenth century, Romanticism, combined the individual expression of emotion and sentimentality with the rejection of strict classical rules, and often led to the development of nationalist themes. For Romantic artists and writers, the individual liberalism characterised by the Enlightenment and revolutionary thinkers and the emotional expression of patriotic nationalism was a powerful combination. Writers such as Heinrich Heine, Benjamin Constant and Johann Gottfried Herder developed the theory of individual equality and national self-determination which increasingly appealed to the educated elite throughout Europe. Two examples of Italian Romantic writing in praise of the nation appear in the case study (see Documents 2.2 and 2.3). They call for Italian national unification and praise the glory of Italy.

This is not to say that the illiterate were not susceptible to nationalist ideas, and that purely emotional arguments did not remain powerful. Indeed the school of Romanticism produced a great deal of nationalist art, literature and even music during the early decades of the nineteenth century which could potentially appeal to all classes. Goya's painting *3 May 1808* (see illustration below), painted in 1814, is a typical example – a call on the emotions of the Spanish to make them identify with the nationalistic rebels being brutally massacred by

Goya, *3 May 1808* (Prado, Madrid). Goya's painting, produced at the request of the Spanish government in 1814, depicts the execution of the people of Madrid by Napoleon's soldiers. The expressions of the victims, one dressed in white with his arms out in the shape of a cross, suggest that they are defiant martyrs for the Spanish nation. In what way do paintings such as *3 May 1808* contribute to the development of nationalism?

Napoleon's troops after they resisted the imposition of Joseph Bonaparte as king of Spain. Frédéric Chopin's Polonaises, composed in the second quarter of the nineteenth century, were named after his country and became a symbol of growing Polish national sentiment.

From these ideas and sentiments grew the nationalist movements which would come to dominate European politics and gradually destroy the Europe temporarily reinstated by the treaty of Vienna. It was significant that the opposition to the established order developed along national lines – Polish, Italian, German, Irish and so on – rather than merely as liberal opposition within the existing state structure. In the early years following Napoleon's defeat, organised nationalist movements remained fairly small and elitist and had limited success in attracting effective popular political support. While the majority of the population may have had some sympathy for nationalist sentiments, fatigue from the long years of war meant that they were not yet prepared to join and participate actively for national liberation. Nationalism was far from being the mass movement it would become by mid-century.

Liberalism and nationalism

The unwillingness and inability of the absolutist regimes to undertake any kind of liberal reform meant that the increasing numbers supporting liberalisation gradually turned towards active outbreaks of protest, which became more and more frequent. Although the Polish insurrection of 1830 collapsed under Russian pressure, the successful revolutions in Belgium and France that same year brought a limited degree of liberalisation and gave hope to many European nationalists that change was possible. In their wake, secret societies such as Young Italy, Young Ireland and Young Germany, grouping together the leading nationalists and reformers from elite intellectual circles, spread through Europe in the early 1830s.

The concrete results of these protests were limited in the short term. The secret societies remained small, relatively weak and essentially ineffective. In spite of the change from a Bourbon to an Orleanist regime in France, the constitutional monarchy remained essentially conservative, and as unwilling as the absolute monarchies had been to allow any real electoral reform. The authorities feared the growing discontent among the lower middle classes who could not yet vote, and a possible repetition of 1789. The economic modernisation and social changes which had come to much of Europe from the Industrial Revolution, increased literacy and a more widely circulated press did nothing but increase the demand for reform. Thus all over continental Europe demand for change was growing, and the kind of liberal reform desired was increasingly associated with change along national lines as middle-class reformers sought to mobilise the support of their fellow countrymen.

As unrest and frustration with the inflexibility of the European monarchies increased, the calls for change and liberation grew louder, outbursts of violence and protest became more frequent, and it was increasingly obvious that progress could only be attained through revolution. During the 1840s most of European society, from the rulers to the peasants, awaited the explosion that was finally to come in 1848. The years 1846–48 were years of poor harvests, and the resulting widespread hunger had led to peasant unrest and brought tension to breaking point. In early 1848, revolution spread through France, Italy, Germany and the Austro-Hungarian Empire like wildfire, toppling regimes and reshaping the political situation almost overnight. The 1848 revolutions were known as the 'Springtime of Peoples' – because for the first time modern nations asserted themselves throughout most of central Europe, and because the benefits, like spring, did not last long. They were, however, the first major sign of the powerful influence popular nationalism was to have on European history.

1848

The revolutions of 1848 themselves achieved little in terms of concrete change. Victory came rapidly all across Europe as the existing regimes collapsed after offering little real resistance, and within a few short months the initial fighting and demonstrations were over and the national celebrations under way. In Germany and Italy it was hoped that revolution would bring about national unification, and in Austria-Hungary that the different nations would emerge independent and egalitarian. The enthusiasm generated and the dreams of social and political change anticipated were as optimistic as the new order was short lived. Outside France, only Hungary and a few parts of Italy were still controlled by revolutionary movements by the winter of 1848–49, and by the summer of 1849 all the former rulers were back in place. The Austrian army had been able to regroup and take Vienna relatively easily by force, and their victory restored the confidence of the king of Prussia and the other German princes, who quickly returned to power. In France, the Second Republic's first assembly to be elected by universal male suffrage, in April 1848, was strongly conservative. The regime itself continued to exist until Napoleon III's *coup d'état* in December 1851, but the momentum of change had already been lost. The only solid accomplishment to emerge from the revolutions was the abolition of serfdom in the Austro-Hungarian Empire, eliminating the last vestiges of the feudal system in western Europe.

The primary significance of the 1848 revolutions was to assert strongly the principle of nationality as a powerful force in Europe, and to shake enough fear of further 'national' uprisings into the existing ruling order to encourage them to implement reforms in the subsequent years. Once they were faced with the uncertainty and chaos of unstable revolutionary assemblies and the breakdown of the forces maintaining order, the middle classes of Europe were revealed to be far more conservative than their liberal and national demands had indicated. They did not give up their national ideals and aspirations, however. In the two decades following 1848, Germany and Italy were unified as nations; and, after some years of protest, Hungary was accorded its own national assembly, distinct from Austria.

It will be revealing at this point to look at Italian and German national unification in greater detail, in order to get some idea of how nationalism shaped the destinies of those two countries.

Italian unification

Dominated by Austria and internally divided into numerous states and principalities, Italy at the beginning of the nineteenth century was no more than 'a geographical expression', in the words of the Austrian chancellor Clemens von Metternich. The Italian nationalists, looking back with nostalgia to former greatness, hoped to bring about the triple goal of national unity, constitutional liberty and independence for the whole of the Italian peninsula. In the pre-1848 years, theirs was far from being a popular movement. Successive armed revolts by an elite minority operating through secret societies began as early as 1820, and were soundly defeated by Austria. Such leaders as Giuseppe Mazzini, the founder of Young Italy, were unable to provoke mass uprisings, but did increase general sympathy for the ideal of Italian national unity. The two texts by Ugo Foscolo and Vincenzo Gioberti (see Documents 2.2 and 2.3) illustrate the kind of nationalist writing, stressing opposition to foreign domination, that was characteristic of the Italian nationalists of the early period.

By the 1840s, frustrated with the failure of the overly Romantic and ineffectual armed revolts, some Italian nationalists began to seek other, more practical ways of bringing about unification than armed uprisings. The first method was the development of economic links between the different states through the construction of the first railways joining the different parts of Italy together, and through the encouragement of common economic and tariff policies. On a political level, different solutions were proposed, such as an association of constitutional monarchies under the leadership of the pope, but nothing could be done as long as Austria retained its powerful divisive influence. During the revolutions of 1848 it was briefly hoped that the triple goal of unity, liberty and independence could be achieved, but this required the co-operation of the different princes and the defeat of the Austrian army. Early victories set up liberal constitutions, but fears of more radical revolts and the refusal to call on France for help led to Italian defeat by Austria, the revocation of all but the Piedmontese constitution and the return to a divided Italy. In the following years, the Piedmontese prime minister Camillo Cavour secured an alliance with Napoleon III of France, who was in favour of a European state system founded upon the rights of peoples and national independence. With the help of the French, the Austrians were finally defeated in 1859. The result was the unification of the principalities of northern Italy in 1861. By 1871 all of the remaining regions had agreed, through plebiscite, to join the constitutional monarchy ruled by Victor-Emmanuel II. Italy had become a unified nation.

German unification

The 39 independent states of Germany – loosely associated by an ancient and almost powerless confederation, but united by a common language and by cultural traditions – were the home of a significant group of nationalist intellectuals calling for unification during the nineteenth century. It was not a simple process, however. The states differed greatly in size, were divided not only politically but in some cases economically, and the whole union was subject to a great deal of Austrian influence which was hostile to integration. In the period after 1814, several of the German states acquired constitutions and were followed in increasing numbers by others after the positive example of the 1830 revolution in France. Among intellectual circles, nationalistic ideas had become increasingly popular. 'German' historical studies developed under the leadership of Leopold von Ranke; and literature, poetry and music expressed this new patriotic feeling emotionally. At first, however, Frederick William III of Prussia (the largest of the German states) was much more concerned with conserving Prussian unity, maintaining absolutism and protecting his alliance with Austria than he was with German unification, especially if unification meant a constitution. Although his attitude prevented any progress towards political union, he was in favour of closer economic ties and proceeded to negotiate the removal of internal customs barriers.

By 1834 most of the German states had joined the customs union known as the *Zollverein*, and in 1838 a single German currency was adopted. During the 1840s agitation in favour of change increased, and when the revolution came in 1848 a parliament was elected with representatives from the whole of Germany. Because of the linguistic and cultural link, some German nationalists considered that Austria itself should become part of a united German nation, but this proved impracticable and they settled for the unification of the rest of the German states. The parliament offered the new imperial crown to Frederick William IV of Prussia. His refusal to accept it, along with a constitution, fatally weakened the parliament, and he and the other German princes were able to regain power and return to the former situation.

Frederick William's victory over the insurgents led him to ask the other princes to give him the crown he had refused from the parliament, but hesitation, coupled with the opposition of Austria and Russia, led him to back down. The next 20 years saw Prussia increase in power as Austria declined; Prussia gradually attracted or compelled first the northern, and then the southern, German states to join Prussia in a united Germany. This required a great deal of skilled negotiation on the part of the Prussian prime minister, Otto von Bismarck, as well as wars with Denmark in 1864, Austria in 1866 and France in 1870–71; the last two of these opponents clearly hoped to preserve a divided Germany. After Prussian military and diplomatic victories, Bismarck secured a constitution for a new German Empire united under William I, which was finally achieved through Prussian domination rather than through compromise.

Thus, from the French Revolution up to 1870, European nationalist movements were closely associated with the doctrine of liberalism. The founding of nations implied the liberation of peoples from the authoritarian domination of absolute monarchy and empire, and was linked to the setting up of constitutions enshrining the rights and duties of the people. Nations were often each other's allies in the common struggle for national unity and freedom from absolutism.

This vision of the nation was illustrated by Eugène Delacroix in 1830 in his painting *Liberty guiding the people*, portraying the female spirit of liberty leading the revolutionary fighting with flag held high (see illustration below). By 1870 most of the absolute monarchies of Europe had been either defeated or restricted by a constitution, and Europe had been reorganised into a continent of nation-states. The process had required patience and many years of struggle, and was achieved through a combination of the use of force, diplomatic activity on the part of the middle and lower middle classes, and popular revolution. While the masses did participate in the revolutions of 1848, nationalism throughout this period was chiefly restricted to the educated classes, and could not be considered a popular movement.

After 1870, however, nationalism was to take a different direction and truly become a mass phenomenon. Nations would no longer be essentially defined simply as 'the people' in opposition to an absolutist monarch, but increasingly in terms of particular national characteristics that would serve to differentiate the nation from other nations. The war against absolutism being more or less won, nations were no longer pure allies in the greater struggle. They became rivals,

Eugène Delacroix, *Liberty guiding the people, 28 July 1830* (Louvre, Paris). Intending to portray the idea that the spirit behind the revolutionary fighting was in fact liberty for the people and thus the nation, Delacroix's painting contains a great deal of national symbolism. Identify some examples of the 'patriotic' or 'national' elements of the painting and explain how you think it could contribute to the nationalist argument.

and defined themselves not versus a king, but versus each other. At the same time, in order to recruit the support of the popular masses, the nations engaged in a complicated process of self-definition which would draw much more upon the emotional attachment to the nation than the rational, legalistic concept which had preoccupied the nationalist thinkers of the first part of the century.

The next two chapters will deal with the various ways in which nations developed their national mythologies and defined their national characteristics. Those chapters will aim to characterise the different historical models for national definition that could be found in Europe.

Document case study

Romantic nationalism

2.1 Excerpt from Johann Gottlieb Fichte, *Addresses to the German nation* (1807–08)

I speak for Germans simply, of Germans simply, not recognising, but setting aside completely and rejecting, all the dissociating distinctions which for centuries unhappy events have caused in this single nation . . . It is only by means of the common characteristic of being German that we can avert the downfall of our nation which is threatened by its fusion with foreign peoples, and win back again an individuality that is self-supporting and quite incapable of any dependence upon others . . .

Now in making this proposal my address is directed especially towards the educated classes in Germany, for I hope that it will be intelligible to them first . . . Now, for the first time, therefore, it happens that the fundamental reconstruction of the nation is offered as a task to the educated classes . . . We shall find that these classes cannot calculate how long it will still remain in their power to place themselves at the head of this movement, since it is now almost prepared and ripe for proposal to the people and is being practised on individuals from among the people; and the people will soon be able to help themselves without any assistance from us. The result of this for us will simply be that the present educated classes and their descendants will become the people; while from among the present people another more highly educated class will arise.

. . .

These addresses should lead you first of all, and with you the whole nation, to a clear perception of the remedy which I have proposed for the preservation of the German nation.

. . .

In the first place, the German is a branch of the Teutonic race . . .

The first and immediately obvious difference between the fortunes of the Germans and the other branches which grew from the same root is this: the former remained in the original dwelling-places of the ancestral stock, whereas the latter emigrated to other places; the former retained and developed the original language of the ancestral stock, whereas the latter adopted a foreign language and gradually reshaped it in a way of their own . . .

The first consequence of that fundamental difference . . . [is] this: among the people with a living language, mental culture influences life, whereas among a people of the opposite kind mental culture and life go their separate ways . . .

. . . [T]he German spirit is an eagle, whose mighty body thrusts itself on high and soars on strong and well-practised wing into the empyrean, that it may rise nearer to the sun whereon it delights to gaze . . .

The Germans who remained in the motherland had retained all the virtues of which their country had formerly been the home – loyalty, uprightness, honour, and simplicity . . . There arose among them . . . cities erected by members of the people. In these cities every branch of culture quickly developed into the fairest bloom. In them arose civic constitutions and organisations which, though but on a small scale, were none the less of high excellence; and, proceeding from them, a picture of order and a love of it spread throughout the rest of the country . . . The monuments of their architecture are standing at the present day and have defied the ravages of centuries; before them posterity stands in admiration and confesses its own importance . . .

The history of Germany, of German might, German enterprise and inventions, of German monuments and the German spirit – the history of all these things during that period is nothing but the history of those cities; and everything else . . . is unworthy of mention.

. . . [W]e have indicated and proved from history the characteristics of the Germans as an original people, and as a people that has the right to call itself simply the people, in contrast to the other branches that have been torn away from it . . .

Source: J. G. Fichte, *Addresses to the German nation*, trans. R. F. Jones and G. H. Turnbull, Chicago and London, 1922

2.2 Excerpt from Ugo Foscolo, *Les Dernières Lettres de Jacopo Ortis* [The final letters of Jacopo Ortis], Letter LXVI, 1802

Italy! Sacred land! On all sides you are encircled with high barriers, and yet they have not stopped being broken through by the unrelenting avarice of the nations. Where are your children? Ah! You are only lacking the force which is born of agreement. Therefore I will gloriously sacrifice my unhappy existence for you. But what can the arm and the feeble voice of one man alone do? What has happened to the terror that your glory transmitted in times gone by? How unfortunate we are! We cannot stop remembering the glory and the freedom of our ancestors; but the more your brilliance shines, the more it uncovers our abject servitude. While we call upon these magnanimous shadows, our proud enemies trample upon their graves, and perhaps the day will come, when, loosing at the same time possessions, spirit and voice, we will become like unto the domestic slaves of the ancients, when we will be sold like Negroes. We will see our masters open up the tombs of our great men, rip out their respected ashes and throw them to the wind, in order to destroy them.

Source: A. Biedermann (ed.), *Le Romantisme européen*, Paris, 1972, pp. 133–5; trans. T. Baycroft

2.3 Excerpt from Vincenzo Gioberti, *Du primat moral et civil des Italiens* [On the moral and civil primacy of Italians], II, xi, 1843

What more beautiful image can be fed to an Italian soul than one of his homeland unified, strong, powerful, devoted to God, calm, confident in itself, respected and admired by other peoples? What more radiant future can be imagined for her? What bliss more desirable? . . .

I imagine my beautiful homeland as one by language, by letters, by religion, by her national genius, by her scientific thought, by the morality of her citizens, by the public and private concordance between the different states and the inhabitants that make them up. I imagine her powerful and unanimous, thanks to a stable and perpetual alliance between her well-loved princes, an alliance which, increasing the force of everyone through the agreement of all, will unify their troops into one national Italian army, will safeguard the peninsula's boundaries from foreign invasion and thanks to a unified navy will make itself fearsome on the seas as well, and will share with the other maritime powers the domination of the ocean . . .

I see the eyes of Europe and the world fixed on this reborn Italy. I see the other nations, surprised at first, but then won over and attentive, receiving from her, in one spontaneous movement, the principles of truth, the rules of beauty, the example and the norms of virtuous action and noble sentiments.

Source: A. Biedermann (ed.), *Le Romantisme européen*, Paris, 1972, pp. 133–5; trans. T. Baycroft

Document case-study questions

1 Why was Document 2.1 directed to the educated classes, and what is their role in the development of the nation?
2 Compare and contrast the descriptions of their respective nations in Documents 2.1 and 2.2.
3 Analyse the sentiments which make up the patriotism in Documents 2.1–2.3.

3 History, popular will and the nation

In this chapter we shall begin to make an analysis of the different ways to define a nation, and of the ways in which the sentiment of nationalism began to spread through all layers of European society. In order for nationalism to pass from a reformist or revolutionary ideology of an intellectual (or at least educated) elite to an ideology of the masses, the idea of the nation itself had to be transformed. To win over the bulk of its population, each nation needed to develop its own image and refine it to make it attractive and appealing to all. This meant that national symbols and emotional links to the nation had to be stressed more than the abstract legalistic concepts that were so crucial to the French revolutionaries. The formation of the national images across Europe varied somewhat from country to country, but did follow some kind of similar pattern.

National history

A key element in every example of European nationalism is the role of history in the formation of the national image. Every nation or would-be nation has a strong identification and association with the past. This can be a glorious past, in which the prestige of the nation and its cultural or military successes was stressed; or, alternatively, a martyred past in which the true nation was kept down by the tyranny and oppression of 'others' outside the nation. While the variety of national histories is great, the importance of the national history in the formation, strengthening and ultimate penetration of national sentiment and nationalism to the roots of the members of the nation cannot be overemphasised. What needs to be examined is the origin of these national histories, the historical content they relate and the way in which they became popularised.

The first point to note is that national sentiment and nationalism do not arise instantaneously; they must be cultivated and encouraged until they gain widespread acceptance by the mass of the population. Nor do national historical myths and the image which the members of a nation have of themselves come ready made; they need to be created. This process requires a great deal of time, using a carefully edited version of the history of the nation which highlights certain key episodes and events and downplays or ignores others. The creation of such a national image requires a selection and interpretation of historical facts, sometimes even a distortion of these facts. Ernest Renan describes the importance of the re-creation or the reinterpretation of history in order to suit national needs and foster national sentiment (see Document 3.1). He goes even further and says that in order for a nation to exist, not only must its history be selective, but forgetting and even historical error are necessary for the formation of a national mythology. Negative images, embarrassing or shameful moments in the nation's history, if they were remembered clearly, might do damage to the nation's credibility.

Equally, the defining characteristics of the nation – be they cultural, ethnic or historic – must be selected and prioritised. In this way one nation may be defined principally by race, another by religion, another by language and another by geography (all those who live on one side of a given mountain range or river, for example). Although in most cases some combination of these factors will be used, the particular characteristics which have been selected as the central features of a given nation will distinguish it in nature from other nations. The combination of particular characteristics is backed up and reinforced by the select interpretation of history. The idea is to show how the members have all lived through and share a similar past, and to demonstrate that these characteristics have unified and continue to unify the identified group into what should be called a nation. The destiny of the group of individuals is portrayed as directly linked to this historical interpretation, this national myth.

Imagined communities

The fact that nations must be individually defined, created and developed raises the question of the existence of the nation before national consciousness. Does the nation truly exist independently of the myths and representations of it? Can one say that a given group of people, based on their obvious similarities, simply ought to be considered by themselves and by others as a nation? One important interpretation claims that it is nationalism and nations which come first, and that the reality of a body of people who share the national characteristics defined by the nation in question, and who identify strongly with them, comes only after the popularisation of a particular national point of view about their history. The national myth precedes the reality of those who accept and identify with it. It is therefore this identification, this consciousness of belonging to the group, and the ability to identify the other members of the group, that leads to the establishment of nations. As Renan says in his speech, some nations are diverse mixes of people who consider themselves to be a nation, while other homogeneous areas are not nations because they lack the consciousness that they are all members of an identifiable group and, more importantly, the popular will to recognise one another as members of the same community. In such situations no claim to 'national' sovereignty is ever asserted. The awareness and acceptance of the historical myth is the overriding central feature of this interpretation of what it means to be a nation.

In this sense nations are imagined communities, created out of the image that the members of the nation create for and of themselves, and based around a historical myth which is as much an artificial creation as a true portrayal of the history of the nation or the people. The principle which is used to define a particular nation is therefore dependent upon the particular group in question and on how they have chosen to view and define themselves, how they interpret their past, and what characteristics they select to define membership of the national group. It is even possible for groups not linked by any recognisable cultural or ethnic feature to consider themselves a nation because they all adhere to the historical myth that they are one, an example being Switzerland.

The nature of the process of historical interpretation, selection, remembrance and forgetting that leads to the creation of a national image or myth is crucial to the understanding of nationalism. Which elements of the past are remembered and which forgotten, which symbols chosen and which discarded? It can be shown that some kinds of historical events and memories are better suited to the creation and enhancement of national sentiment and nationalism than others, which it is better to forget. In this latter category are such events as civil wars; conquests of one part of the now integral territory by another; and any kind of tension – be it religious, linguistic, territorial, commercial, ethnic or otherwise – between groups now considered (or desired) to be members of the same nation. Those elements that do lend themselves to historical glorification of the nation include battles won by the forces of the antecedents of the would-be nation; historical figures considered to be heroes and great patriots at the same time; and any former political states (whether kingdoms or empires) or integral but oppressed regions, even if they made only a brief appearance on the historical scene before disappearing completely. In this way Flemish nationalists associate themselves with the county of Flanders, which has not been independent since the thirteenth century, and the French claim roots in the pre-Roman Gaul of Vercingetorix. The current or would-be nation must glorify its association with historical battles, figures and territories. It goes without saying that the older and greater this particular kind of identification, the better.

National symbols

When describing or promoting the historical events that are positive for the nation, it is often useful to associate them with a series of symbols which do not come directly out of events in the history of the nation, but which are in many ways impartial, vague signifiers. Symbols such as national animals – the Russian bear, the Austrian eagle, the Flemish lion, the French rooster – can all be used to promote the nation, even to personify the nation in its better moments, without directly evoking painful or potentially controversial historical memories.

A good example to illustrate this practice comes from France, and relates to the way in which the national leaders selected the date for a national holiday and chose symbols commemorating the French Revolution and the establishment of a republic in France. The final choice of national holiday, made in 1880 under the Third Republic, was for 14 July, commemorating the taking of the Bastille by the people of Paris. This was an ideal choice; it symbolised the fall of an institution representing the old regime, opposed to the 'nation' of the people, but one which was relatively insignificant at the time (there was only a handful of unimportant prisoners in the Bastille when it was taken by the revolutionary mob). If the date chosen had been, say, the anniversary of the execution of Louis XVI (21 January), it would have alienated a large segment of the population: the descendants of the aristocracy and the royalist regions, all of whom had some negative memories associated with the guillotine and the Terror. That kind of memory would have divided the people of France and was better left forgotten. Bastille day could raise no such objection because it was, as we have seen, a celebration of an incident without strongly divisive emotional undercurrents; all could identify with it, or at least find it inoffensive.

A similar approach can be seen in the choice of Marianne to symbolise the republic (see illustration below). Here was a national symbol which could be put up on the front of the city halls in all the French towns, and which could not offend anyone because it was not linked to anything in particular. Because of this all of the good, the glory, the ideals and the essence of the nation that had been consciously and selectively drawn from its history could be projected onto this symbol, and used to promote the national cause. The ambiguity of the symbol itself contributes to its success.

The national flag is another way to promote nationalism through history with little risk of evoking dangerous memories. After the fall of Napoleon III, one factor

This image portrays Marianne, the female incarnation of the French Republic, in a pose that reminds the viewer of royalty. Why is Marianne a useful symbol for a nation?

in the choice of regime to follow him was the question of which flag was to be used. The comte de Chambord's refusal to come to the throne unless the white Bourbon flag was readopted eventually meant that the monarchy was never re-established. The flag that was chosen, the tricolour, represented the positive elements of the liberal heritage and the French 'nation'; the Bourbon flag symbolised only the king and the monarchy, leaving out the French people. The flags were linked to particular political regimes, but in themselves they are as meaningless as Marianne; they simply take on the historical connotations which are attributed to them. They have a flexibility that allows a specific interpretation of history to be attributed to and associated with them.

The positive promotion of a nation in all its regions through the widespread portrayal of its images and symbols reminds the population of their historical links. Those links, as we have seen, may be selected to represent the way the promoters of the nation wish the nation to be seen and thought of. Thus every time a French person sees a French national flag or a statue of Marianne, they will be reminded of the historical events associated with it. Memories of events which emphasise the negative aspects of the history of the formation of the modern nation will not be evoked. The national symbols draw from history in specific ways, and allow for the kind of historical forgetting of the negative sides of the revolution (the Terror) that Renan has said is necessary for the formation of nations and national myths.

Historical figures

Further examples of the selective use of history can be found in the way historical figures are portrayed. In the uncertain political climate of France in the late nineteenth century, overemphasis of any of the revolutionary, or more recent, figures would have given too much weight to particular political viewpoints and been divisive rather than unifying. Danton, Robespierre, the other revolutionaries and, to some extent, Napoleon were glorified as a group, but downplayed as individuals. The individuals on whom accent was placed were non-political figures such as Marianne and heroes from the more distant past. The further removed from the present they were, the smaller the risk of the heroes evoking unpleasant memories and the easier it was to edit their achievements. Such national heroes as Joan of Arc find their place in the national mythology; even republican nationalists stress her loyalty, her patriotism and her desire to promote and to save her country, at the same time disregarding the fact that she was a supporter of the king and the Roman Catholic church. French nationalists also claim the glories of Louis XIV and other French kings for the nation, apparently forgetting that they were authoritarian kings, opposed to the type of government by the people that was advocated by republican France in the latter part of the nineteenth century. When it comes to the lives of particular national heroes or heroines, therefore, Renan's comment that many things must be remembered and others forgotten in order for nationalism to develop remains applicable.

National events

In some cases history is not only edited in order to further the development of nationalism, but in effect invented in order to suit national ends. Official state ceremonies such as coronations, inaugurations and commemorations are sometimes developed in order to raise the profile of the nation, and to give an impression of longevity, stability and historical tradition which is fictitious. This has become known as 'inventing traditions'. This kind of national ceremony provides a festive atmosphere, one of celebration and enjoyment, at the same time creating an apparent link to the past, to the 'historical traditions' of the nation. In reality these links may be dubious or indeed fictitious. In such cases the traditions are not even selected interpretations of the past, but are clearly inventions intended to give the nation an air of history, of continuity with the past – even when the ceremony in question is not historic and has never been held before. Examples abound across Europe, from the construction of the Bismarck columns of the German Empire and the jubilees of various European monarchies to the issuing of commemorative postage stamps. These events may highlight the current nation and suggest where its roots are. Thus invented traditions have a part in the connections between the nation, nationalism and history.

For all nations seeking to promote and advance nationalism, therefore, history has an important role to play. The manner in which it is used is selective, and memory and forgetting are both integral parts of the formation of the national myth and the national image. Each nation uses history in its own way in order to develop the kind of image it has made of itself.

The spread of symbols

We have discussed the national myth derived from a selective interpretation of history, through which the members of the nation collectively remember and identify with certain events of history and forget others. Something must now be said about the way in which a large group of people comes to identify with the same national image – the way in which national myths spread through and gain wide acceptance among the general populace of the nation. Here again the role of history is of primary importance. The extent to which national history is taught in schools, communicated in speeches and spread by the written word will influence the degree of popular national consciousness. Education is particularly significant in popularising and solidifying national sentiment in a pre-existing state structure (such as France or Spain) and among the regions of newly unified countries (for example, Italy and Germany). In these areas the state education system can teach 'national' history, which is an extremely effective way of promoting the national image to the mass of the population and to cultivate the will to further the development of the nation.

Where the would-be nation is not an existing state, but believes that it should be able to form a state of its own, it is through regional education and regional history, and through unofficial channels such as speeches, pamphlets, newspapers and the word of mouth, that the image is passed on and developed. The popularisation of history through education goes hand in hand with increased consciousness of the national myths, the will to form and belong to nations and the rise of nationalism.

Popular will

Another major concept that arises out of Renan's text is the idea that a nation is a group of people who desire to be together and consider themselves to be a nation. It is popular will that decides which group is a nation and which is not, rather than race or religion, language or any of the other criteria that can be used to define a given nation. Will is linked to history but it means that, in theory at least, anyone who wishes to be considered a member of a nation and is desired by the others to be part of it can be a member; no other criterion limits the possibility of membership. Since, as Renan writes, the people come together by means of a widespread decision and mutual recognition of the fact that they belong together, it is possible for others to come from outside and join, provided that the national myth is of the kind that can be adapted to fit newcomers. The idea of citizenship as a central feature of a nation can be flexible in this way. Immigrants who arrive in the country, provided they adhere to the principles of the nation, can in theory be eventually accepted as a part of it and become full citizens and members.

This is often called 'civic nationalism' and is most frequently identified with France. In many ways it acknowledges the role of history and the role of will in the formation and identity of a nation, and does not consider that nations can exist independently of national myths and national consciousness. This is because the particular defining principle of the French nation is a reasonably or relatively flexible one, still based in part upon the legal, rational concept of the nation championed during the French Revolution, as discussed in Chapter 1. The same does not apply to all nations; much depends upon which elements have been used as the basis for the national mythology and as the central features of nationhood. If as the defining principle the nation emphasises criteria which are exclusive, this kind of immigration and flexibility may not be possible. The role of interpretative history and forgetting is, however, integral to the formation of every national image. In the next chapter we shall turn to two other key concepts in the development and popularisation of the nation and nationalism in the latter part of the nineteenth century: culture and ethnicity.

The political construction of national mythologies

3.1 Excerpt from *What is a nation?*, a speech by Ernest Renan at the Sorbonne in Paris, 11 March 1882

I propose to analyse with you an idea, clear and straightforward in appearance, but which lends itself to the most dangerous of misunderstandings . . . At the time of the French Revolution, it was believed that the institutions of small independent cities such as Sparta and Rome could be applied to our large nations with between thirty and forty thousand souls. In our day, we are committing a more serious error: we are confusing race and nation, and attributing to ethnic or rather linguistic groups the kind of sovereignty analogous to that of peoples which really exist. Let us attempt to find some precision in these difficult questions . . . We will do so with the most absolute detachment and impartiality.

. . .

Forgetting and, I would even say, historical error are an essential factor in the creation of a nation, and thus the advances of historical study are often threatening to a nationality. Historical investigation, in fact, brings to light the acts of violence that have taken place at the origin of every political formation, even those whose consequences have been the most beneficial. Unity is always created through brutality: the unification of northern and southern France was the result of continual exterminations and terror lasting for almost a century . . .

Now the essence of a nation is that individuals have many things in common, but also that they have forgotten many other things. No French citizen knows if he is Burgundian, Alani, Taifali or Visigoth; every French citizen must have forgotten St Bartholomew's Day, the thirteenth-century massacres in the Midi.

The modern nation is therefore a historical result brought about by a series of phenomena converging in the same direction. Sometimes unity has been brought about by a dynasty, as is the case with France; sometimes by the direct will of the provinces, as is the case with Holland, Switzerland and Belgium; sometimes by a general sensibility, belatedly conquering the caprices of feudalism, as is the case with Italy and Germany . . . The principles in such cases come to light only by the most unexpected surprises. It is France's glory to have proclaimed, through the French Revolution, that a nation exists by itself. What then is a nation? Why is Holland a nation, whereas Hanover or the Grand Duchy of Parma is not? How is it that Switzerland, which has three languages, two religions and three or four races, is a nation, whereas Tuscany, for example, which is so homogeneous, is not? . . . How does the principle of nationality differ from the principle of race?

. . .

A nation is a spiritual principle resulting from the profound complications of history, a spiritual family and not a group determined by the configuration of the land. We have seen what is insufficient to create such a spiritual principle: race, language, interests, religious affinity, geography and military exigencies. What else then is required? . . .

A nation is a soul, a spiritual principle. Two things, which strictly speaking are just one, constitute this soul, this spiritual principle. One is the past, the other the present. One is the common possession of a rich legacy of memories; the other is actual consent, the desire to live together, the will to continue to value the heritage that has been received in common . . . The nation, like the individual, is the outcome of a long and strenuous past of sacrifice and devotion. Of all cults, the cult of ancestors is the most legitimate, since our ancestors have made us what we are. A heroic past of great men, of glory . . . : this is the social capital on which a national ideal is established . . .

A nation is therefore the expression of a great solidarity, constituted by a feeling for the common sacrifices that have been made and for those one is prepared to make again. It presupposes a past; however, it is epitomised in the present by a tangible fact: consent, the clearly expressed desire that the common life should continue. The existence of a nation is (excuse the metaphor) a daily plebiscite, just as the existence of the individual is a perpetual affirmation of life . . . In the order of ideas I am placing before you, a nation has no more right than a king to say to a province: 'You belong to me, therefore, I am taking you.' A province, for us, is its inhabitants, and if anyone has the right to be consulted in this matter, it is the inhabitant. A nation never has a genuine interest in annexing or retaining a country against its will.

. . .

Man is the slave neither of his race, his language, nor his religion; neither of the courses of the rivers, nor the mountain ranges. One great aggregate of men, of sound spirit and warm heart, creates a moral conscience that is called a nation. In so far as this moral conscience proves its strength through the sacrifices demanded by the renunciation of the individual for the good of the community, it is legitimate and has the right to exist.

Source: E. Renan, 'Qu'est-ce qu'une nation?', in *Qu'est-ce qu'une nation? et autres essais politiques*, Paris, 1992; trans. T. Baycroft

Document case-study questions

1 **Why is forgetting an essential part of nation-building?**
2 **In what sense can a nation be considered a spiritual principle?**
3 **What is meant by the phrase 'a daily plebiscite'?**

Culture, ethnicity and the nation

In addition to having a historically based national mythology, as we saw in the preceding chapter, a would-be nation needs to emphasise some common cultural elements as parts of its national identity in order to engage the popular masses with the idea of the nation. A shared culture which can be called national is essential, both as a means of transmitting national values and as a key element in the national image itself. This chapter will begin by examining the role which culture played in the popularisation of the idea of the nation and nationalism in the latter stages of the nineteenth century, and will go on to examine the links between culture and ethnicity, another key element in the creation of national self-images.

National languages

The most common cultural element which binds a national culture together is language. Language provides a means of communicating between people, and an easy means of identifying others who are 'like' oneself – they speak in the same way. Not every kind of language can fulfil this national role, however; it must be a written one. Writing first of all helps to bring about standardisation, with established rules for grammar and spelling which will guarantee that the language will be the same across the nation – even among those individuals (or communities) who have never met and may not have any direct contact with one another. Writing also permits long-distance communication between citizens and officials, and circulation of messages understandable everywhere within national territory by the central authorities.

It is worth noting that during the nineteenth century the majority of the population was not only not literate, but did not necessarily speak a version of their national language. Many people used a local dialect, often not understandable to those from different regions, or some kind of regional, unwritten language that was maintained purely through oral tradition. The most extreme case was Italy, in which the vast majority of the population spoke Piedmontese, Sicilian or one of the other regional languages. It has been estimated that at the time of unification those who could actually speak Italian made up as little as between 2 and 12 per cent of the population. In France at mid-century the proportion who spoke French was greater, but still only came to about half the population. Thus the first task facing the nations hoping to obtain mass participation was to teach the population their national language as well as the ability to read and to write it. Through that language they would gain access to an important part of the national culture, and hopefully become an active part of the nation.

Schools

The principal means of teaching national languages was of course through education within the school system. Throughout the nineteenth century, the various European states gradually expanded the availability of primary education, increasing the number of schools, decreasing and then removing fees, moving towards the goal of primary education which was free and compulsory for the whole population. The teaching of the national language was only one of the reasons for developing and enhancing primary education; others included the teaching of morality with the hope of decreasing civil unrest and increasing obedience to the laws of the state, and the training of a workforce with skills adapted to the industrial workplace. Integration of the population into the national culture was nevertheless crucial for the nation-states who hoped to preserve the loyalty of their citizens. The schools served to teach not only the national language, but also knowledge of the nation's geography and institutional structure as well as the official version of national history, as we have seen in the previous chapter.

Military service

A secondary means of teaching the national language was through compulsory military service, which would bring together young male citizens from the different regions of the nation, with the national language as their only means of communication. The soldiers were deliberately separated from others of the same locality and put into mixed regiments in order to ensure that the only option available was to use the national language. As a secondary benefit, the years of military service would also provide the men with an opportunity to learn from those around them about other parts of the nation besides their own locality, and hopefully they would as a result come to a greater understanding of what the nation meant. Being in the military would, needless to say, also encourage the kind of loyalty and patriotism that national leaders were seeking to cultivate among the populace. At the end of their military service, the soldiers would return to their villages with a knowledge of the national language and greater familiarity with their nation and its culture.

It seems ironic that it is necessary to teach the people of a nation 'their' culture, but that this is done demonstrates once again the idea of inventing the nation that was described in the previous chapter with respect to national histories. Just as a national history and national traditions needed to be developed and popularised, national cultures needed to be taught. Just after the Italian unification in 1861, Massimo d'Azeglio exclaimed, 'We have made Italy, now we must make Italians.' National languages and national culture were not spread to the masses overnight, but the later nineteenth and early twentieth centuries saw a great deal of progress.

Local or regional cultures are obvious rivals to national languages and cultures. In central Europe the nations which asserted themselves in the nineteenth century did so through the development of their languages and cultures. Nations which did not have a long history as existing states relied even more heavily on their culture as a basis for national identity. Because of this languages such as Czech and Hungarian, which had not previously been literary languages, acquired standardised rules and a rapidly developing literature, and were at the heart of nationalist independence movements. In the larger western states, government policy sought to prevent any regional movements within their borders from developing their language and culture with a view to aspiring to nation status. In both France and Germany, the Roman Catholic church supported the use of some regional languages in opposition to the central authorities, and the governments combined anti-clericalism with nationalism in a battle against the church and potential regionalist rivals. Bismarck's *Kultur-kampf*, or 'culture battle', was waged against the church in a move to strengthen the central authorities throughout the empire. This was especially true for the borderland areas, such as Alsace-Lorraine in the west and the Polish territories acquired by Prussia in the east.

Political integration

While nations strove to increase the use of their national languages, they were also indoctrinating people into the nation through political education and democracy. In those states where the vote existed, the possibilities of this means of cultural transmission were increased as the franchise was extended to include greater numbers. Political culture was inherently national, since local representatives went to national parliaments and the principal parties, issues and policy debates were national ones. Participation in national political life was a good way to attach people to their nation. As they became involved in political issues they thought automatically in national terms, and the fact that they were national was quickly taken for granted and accepted. To popularise nationalism using this kind of political education presupposes that the 'nation' is already synonymous with the state, as it was in most of the western European countries. Beginning in the latter part of the nineteenth century, the existing nation-states began to use political education actively to encourage national loyalty. When the nation hoping to be developed and popularised is not in fact a state, as in several places in eastern Europe and in Ireland, the first and primary demand of nationalists was to have their own state – or at the very least to use the apparatus of state to begin to have their 'national' language taught in schools, with hopes of future statehood.

Associated with both political and linguistic education, the development of the popular press aided the penetration of the national culture into the regions. Written in the national language and containing national news and especially information about national politics, newspapers encouraged citizens to think about and to discuss national matters. The involvement they gave people in the affairs of the nation helped to strengthen the ties of the individuals to their nation.

National institutions and culture

Another significant means for nation-states to integrate their populations into the national culture is by using national institutions and administration. Examples include the symbolism behind the uniforms of state officials and the images appearing on postage stamps, public buildings and official documents – as well as the use of common currency. The law courts and all local branches of administration used the national language and followed national procedures. As state machinery increased in size, and the average citizen's contact with officials and need for documents or authorisation increased, the nation was able to tighten its grip on the rural areas within its boundaries. The apparatus and the symbols of the nation gradually became familiar to all of the population through the efforts of countless local representatives of the state authority, and the necessity of using the national language, both in its written and its oral form, was underlined by the presence of local branches of national institutions and of the administration.

Thus through the spread of the national language and exposure to national institutions, the nation-states of Europe hoped to integrate the masses into their 'national' cultures. To be a member of the nation entailed speaking and reading the national language, and being familiar with the national political system and the geography of the nation. Culture also formed national mentalities. Marcel Mauss, writing in the early 1920s, describes the phenomenon of nation-building which had occurred over the previous 50 years and stresses the idea that nations sought to differentiate themselves culturally and mentally from one another (see Document 4.1). Where previously society had been made up of diverse groups which did not necessarily coincide with the boundaries of the states in which they lived, there was a tendency in the nation-states of the later nineteenth and early twentieth centuries to move towards cultural homogeneity, with all those residing in the same nation speaking the same language and having the same culture.

National cultures were more than vehicles to encourage the integration of the population; they also formed a crucial element in national identities and became values in themselves. Mauss comments that it is a characteristic of modernity to make a language into a 'cult-object' and assert its inherent qualities. In order for the idea of the nation and nationalism to be spread to the masses, some form of sociological transformation of the attitudes towards culture is necessary. Culture is no longer merely a part of one's existence, but becomes a defining feature of one's identity. Furthermore, an individual culture is held to be valuable and 'good' – better than other cultures and a source of pride. If we look back at the texts in Chapter 2 by Fichte, Foscolo and Gioberti (Documents 2.1, 2.2 and 2.3), these sentiments come out clearly. They speak of the glory of their cultures and praise their superiority.

One dimension of culture which can contribute to national identity and has not yet been discussed is religion. While in many nations religion could not and did not play any role in developing a distinct national character, several nations – such as Ireland, Belgium, Serbia, Bosnia and Poland – have defined themselves partly in religious terms. Unlike language and the cultural elements discussed above, this aspect of culture does not need to be 'taught' to the population. The people need only be made aware of how their religion is characteristic of their nation, and therefore that those around them of other religions belong to other nations. This process does require education of a sort, but it is one of linkages and association of ideas. In these cases, religion can add a fervour or urgency to the nationalism that is often more intense than that of other nations developing without a religious dimension.

Ethnicity

Having now examined historical myth and national culture as elements of national identity, it will be useful to have a look at the ways in which race or ethnicity contribute to the definition of nations. The definition of a race, those sharing common blood and descent, is an extension of the natural ties which humans have from their family to a wider group of people. In this way the ethnically defined nation is a 'greater family', seeking to obtain the kind of emotional attachment to the nation naturally felt for one's kin. Ethnicity is partly historical in the sense that the nation traces its roots to common ancestry, and is therefore subject to the same rules of historical forgetting (for example, of migration or ethnic mixing) that were discussed in the previous chapter.

Unlike the concepts of popular will put forward by Renan, or of culture discussed above, both of which imply some degree of choice and active involvement, ethnicity is an inflexible concept. You are either of a certain race or you are not, and no quantity of effort will ever be able to change that. Ethnic definitions of the nation are exclusive, and less flexible than other national models. They postulate much more strongly that the nation pre-exists any consciousness of it, so that whether the people are aware of belonging to the nation or not, indeed whether they wish to or not, they are automatically included in the nation by virtue of their ancestry.

Surprisingly, perhaps, Mauss claims that even race or ethnicity is invented, and comes after the nation (see Document 4.1). The level of interbreeding in all of the European countries means that the French are no more descended from the Gauls than they are from the Turks and that all of the major ethnically defined nations are in reality racially mixed, to the point of being indistinguishable from their neighbours. The reality of interbreeding means that a national history tracing ethnic roots is as much a product of historical selection and forgetting as any other element in a national historical mythology. The ethnic definition of the nation seems at face value more 'natural' or given, for the very reason that no choice appears to be involved. Like the idea of natural boundaries, ethnicity is more difficult to dispute and is seemingly less open to question, which is what makes it such a powerful argument in favour of the nation. We have already seen this kind of national argument in the Fichte text (Document 2.1). Fichte claims that the Germans are not only an original people, but that they have the right to be called '*the* people', understood to be somehow purer and therefore superior to other peoples. Fichte goes to great length to establish the purity of the German ethnic community, with the goal of developing loyalty to the German nation.

With the many ways to define national identity – through history, geography, culture, religion and ethnicity – the objective of nationalists is to define the characteristics of their national group and encourage national consciousness at a popular level. This process implies distinguishing between 'us' and 'them', and identifying those who do not share the national characteristics as rivals. The opposition between rival nations thinking of themselves in terms of us and them is a characteristic feature of the development of nations in the period after 1870. Previously, when the idea of the nation was more closely linked to the legal concept which implied equality for the people in opposition to absolute monarchs, the rivalries between different nations were secondary to the common struggle. Once absolutism was in decline, and nation-states seeking to bring the idea of the nation to the majority of the population came into existence, it was the differences between the nations, their exclusivity and opposition to each other that shaped and defined the growth of nations and nationalism.

As the idea of the nation became popular, the emotional dimension took precedence over the rational, legalistic concept inherited from the French Revolution. The emotional arguments used were persuasive and attractive, encouraging everyone to share in the glory of the nation's past and present achievements, to identify with the nation's virtuous qualities – whether they were historical, ethnic, cultural or any combination of these – and to feel good because they belonged. If any individuals or other nations had wronged their own, they could sympathise with the outrage in the same way that they could share in the glory of the nation as a whole. The idea of the nation did not mean abandonment of the dimension of individual liberties which it had from the beginning, but each nation became exclusive, and the virtue and progressiveness of the original position were extended to all of the qualities of the nation.

During this stage of historical development, nations became increasingly characterised by their individuality and their differences from other nations, each one developing its own unique image and identity. They may have been essentially civic nations (see Chapter 3) or principally ethnic ones, putting greater emphasis on culture, ethnicity, geography, religion or history, but, as Mauss concludes, in mature nations all of these elements of national identity will have been developed to a greater or lesser degree (see Document 4.1). The nation-states developed national images which needed to be invented and adapted to fit the circumstances, and then taught to the people in order to win their loyalty for the nation. These states used their authority to encourage the majority of the population to accept the nation as a part of their identity through education and administrative integration. The largely emotional attachments forged to the abstract and invented ideas of the nation proved to be strong, and loyalty and patriotism followed closely upon the acceptance of national identity.

We shall go on to examine the ways in which, between 1870 and 1914, nationalism evolved after it had become the acknowledged ideology of a new

Europe of nation-states. In preparation for that, we have analysed the concrete political strategies chosen by these new European nation-states to secure the loyalty of their people and to spread the ideology on which their legitimacy was founded: nationalism. We have seen how much popular nationalism had to be constructed by the political powers, and examined the various methods of doing so. It is important to be aware that in each state the process of diffusion required a very specific, conscious and deliberate cultural policy of education and assimilation of the masses. During the second half of the nineteenth century, the idea of the nation penetrated widely into the European population, as it changed from being the ideology of a reforming elite during the French Revolution to become the dominant ideology of the states, involving the majority of their people. The next chapter represents a brief aside in order to look at the ways in which the idea of the nation was challenged by the idea of class during the nineteenth century.

Elements of national identity

4.1 Excerpt from 'Nation, nationality, internationalism' by Marcel Mauss (1920–21)

We now have the idea, utterly foreign to the *ancien régime*, that an individual can serve only his Country [*la patrie*] . . . Everything in a modern nation standardises and individualises its members. Like a primitive clan, it is homogeneous, and is composed of allegedly equal citizens. It is symbolised by its flag, as the clan is by its totem; it has its cult of *la patrie*, just as the clan has its cult of ancestral animal-gods. Like a primitive tribe, its dialect is raised to the level of language, and it has domestic laws that conflict with international law . . . It has its currency, its exchange rates and its credit; it has its customs, its frontiers and its colonies, which it generally lays exclusive claim to exploit, and of which it is also the only governor . . . The thought of a single language, rich in tradition, allusion and sophistication, with a complex syntax, an abundant, ongoing and manifold literature, centuries of reading, writing, education, and, especially in the last fifty years, a daily press; this thought has been universalised to a degree unknown in the highest civilisations, ancient and modern. All this means that the mentality of a Frenchman is even less similar to that of an Englishman, than the mentality of an Algonquian is to that of a Californian Indian. It also means that there is an infinitely greater separation between how an Italian and a Spaniard think and feel, although both come from a single civilisation, than there is in popular morals and imagination, for the extraordinary uniformity across the world of the latter expresses the unity of the primitive human being.

In fact, this individuation in the formation of nations is a significant sociological phenomenon, while its novelty is not usually properly appreciated . . .

Up until modern times, none of the majority groups was characteristic of a given society. Their frontiers, even those of language and law, were not necessarily those of the tribes and the states that used them. They were only exceptionally the object of those beliefs that bring a people to associate themselves with their institutions. Neither Greek nor Latin became a people's cult-object such as French has been since the seventeenth century and the French Academy; as German has been since Lessing and Fichte; and Italian since Dante. In the modern nations, by contrast, all, or a certain number, of the signs we have recognised as being insufficient to define the limits of a society in space and time, can be, especially in the unified nations, the object of that superstitious attraction which, in the most primitive formations, was inspired only by the law and the juridical elements of religion.

A modern nation believes in its race. This is a greatly mistaken belief, however, especially in Europe, where every known population, excepting perhaps the Norse populations and a few Slavs, were of course the product of recent and profuse interbreeding. This does not, however, hinder the Germans, especially since the romantics, from imagining that there exists a German race; Fichte, with swathes of linguistic and philosophical fantasy, took great pains to prove that the Germans alone are an *Urstamm* [a primal tribe: the Teutons] ... Hence the extremely questionable deployment of the so-called 'ethnographic' notions in history, still more dubious in diplomacy ... But all these paradoxes, paralogisms and sophisms of political interest are created by one basic fact that they show up: new races are formed at the core of modern nations ... In short, because the nation created the race, it was believed that the race created the nation. This was simply to extend certain beliefs to the entire populace, that until then had been restricted to the divine race of kings, to the blessed stock of the nobility, and to the castes who had to maintain their pure blood, who had gone so far as consanguineous marriage to ensure it. It is because every last Frenchman or German takes pride in his nation that he has ended up taking pride in his race.

Next, the nation believes in its language ... With the formation of nations, the language of culture becomes popular language, and the emotions of which it used to be the object extend to the people as a whole. Fine talk, linguistic excellence, the distinction between those who speak the language and those who do not; all this has become conventional wisdom. For the average German, every German must speak the high Saxon German that became successively the language of the courts, the language of literature, the language of religion with Luther, that of the military with Frederick and, following the Enlightenment, the language of the university. The history of the French language is the same ... The last century has seen the creation of national languages by peoples who used not to have one ... The Flemish campaign for a University of Ghent, the Ruthenians for a University of Lemberg, the Croats for a University of Agram: these are only the final episodes in the linguistic nationalism of peoples who want to add the colour of their languages to European culture, and who, in order to do this, build up, maintain and perfect a language at the cost of notable stresses and effort.

If, however, the various nationalities do create their own languages, it is because language, in modern times, creates if not the nation, then at least the nationality. The development of great scientific and moral literatures, along with the cast of mind created by identical methods of education on a vigorous and undreamed-of scale, begins to shape a national mentality ... A nation believes in *its* civilisation, in its customs, its industry and fine arts. It teaches its own literature, its sculpture, its science, its techniques, its morals, its tradition; in a word, its character. It is almost always prey to the illusion of being the world's pre-eminent nation. It teaches its literature as if it were the only literature, science as if it alone had contributed to it, its techniques as if it had invented them, and its morals as if they were the best and the most beautiful. In this there is a natural complacency, partly caused by ignorance and political sophism, but in many cases by the exigencies of education. Not even the smallest nations avoid this.

. . .

Briefly, a complete nation is a sufficiently integrated society, with a central power, democratic to a certain extent, having in every case the notion of national sovereignty, and whose frontiers are those of a race, a civilisation, a language, a moral code – in a word, a national character. Certain of these elements may be missing . . . In mature nations, however, all this coincides.

Source: S. Woolf (ed.), *Nationalism in Europe 1815 to the present: a reader*, London, 1996; this extract trans. I. H. Grant. Originally published as 'Nation, nationalité, internationalism', in M. Mauss, Œuvres, vol. 3, *Cohésion sociale et division de la sociologie*, Paris, 1969 [1920–1]

Document case-study questions

1 What is the role of culture in dividing the peoples of Europe?

2 What does the 'individuation' of nations mean?

3 According to Mauss, which comes first, the nation or the nationality, and why?

4 What are the characteristics of a mature nation?

5 Class versus nation

By 1870, the nation-state had become established as the dominant form of political organisation in western Europe. From this time forward, the ruling classes were able to use official policy and the apparatus of the state to put into practice the combined doctrines of moderate nationalism, economic and political liberalism, and social conservatism. Such regimes as the French Third Republic and the united German Empire under Bismarck founded their authority on the will of the nation as it was defined during the French Revolution and claimed the heritage of the nationalist movements of the first half of the nineteenth century. In the final decades of the century, mass support for these nation-states in the form of popular nationalism increased through the means we have seen in the preceding two chapters, but was by no means unanimous or without criticism.

Marxist ideology

At the time that the ideology behind nation-forming and national liberty was expanding through and taking hold of Europe, a rival ideology was also being developed. This, the ideology of class, would oppose the idea of nations and their legality. Often referred to as Marxist ideology, this theory holds that economic and social class is the primary means of understanding human development, and that it is class conflict that brings about progress. While this ideology would be upheld only by a minority excluded from the sphere of power and from the mainstream intellectual circles of Europe, it would nevertheless seriously challenge the nationalist interpretation of history at the heart of the legitimacy of the majority of the European democratic nations. Liberal nationalism remained the ideology of the majority of intellectuals, gradually becoming more and more widespread among the population as well as being the legal basis for state organisation. From the middle of the nineteenth century onwards it would be criticised from the left by the more progressive, reform-minded elements in Europe.

The first major difference between Marxist class theory and the ideology of the nation is their interpretation of history and historical development, especially their analysis of the French Revolution. According to the Marxist interpretation of history, the French Revolution was not a revolution of the nation against the king, but of the middle class or bourgeoisie against the upper class or nobility, as represented by the absolute monarchy and the noble privileges of the *ancien régime*. The evidence for this is that all of the revolutionary leaders, such as

Danton, Robespierre, Jean Paul Marat and Louis Antoine Saint-Just, were professional men (lawyers, doctors, journalists and so on), businessmen or property owners. These members of the educated and wealthy bourgeoisie were frustrated at being excluded from power and influence, and fought to change the power structure of French society to obtain greater control for the middle class.

While the revolution did occasionally permit members of the peasantry or the working classes to better themselves economically and move up the social ladder, they always achieved that by acquiring money or education and becoming bourgeois themselves. As a whole, the Marxists argue, the majority of the people did not benefit directly from the French Revolution; only those members of the middle class who gained power from the demise of the aristocracy gained anything. The revolution was not a 'national' revolution of the French people as a whole, but merely a revolution of the middle class against the upper class. This position was confirmed by the social conservatism of the 'national' regimes that gained power towards the end of the nineteenth century. They may have been economically and politically liberal, but social rigidity protected the wealth and the position of the bourgeoisie, thus preserving the rule and domination of the middle classes.

This class-based interpretation of the French Revolution even questions the idea of the nation as a legal principle. For the nationalists, the nation is the same as the people and is the foundation of all legitimacy and legality (see Chapter 1). The members of the nation are citizens, equal in the eyes of the law. For the Marxists, this equality is nothing but an abstraction or a figure of speech. It does not represent the reality of human existence, which can only be truly understood by an analysis which takes into consideration the socio-economic conditions of daily lives. It is with this perspective that Marxism developed its vision of human history centred not upon the abstract legal philosophy of theoretical equality, but upon the economic laws which govern class behaviour and class conflict, and which describe society in its reality.

In this interpretation of history, the Marxists not only argue that the French Revolution was a class, not a national revolution, but that all major historical change is a result of class conflict – in other words, that class is the motor of history. All societies are divided into those who rule and own, and those who work and serve; and sooner or later the tension between them will turn into conflict between the rich and the poor, the haves and the have-nots. The result of each conflict is that a new equilibrium will be established, and the new economic conditions will then determine the nature of the next conflict. Following the French Revolution, the gradual rise of the nations in the nineteenth century marked, according to Marxist analysis, the consolidation of bourgeois power and its continued domination over the lower classes. Furthermore, the very idea of the nation is an invention of the bourgeois middle classes; in truth it represents only the middle-class interests of the revolutionaries and is used unconsciously to manipulate and dominate the lower classes. They argue that the French Revolution and the rise of the nation represent only one episode in the history of class struggle: the victory of the bourgeoisie.

The proletarian revolution and internationalism

Marxist analysis did not restrict itself to the historical assessment of past phases of the class struggle, but also predicted future conflicts which would lead to the true liberation of the people. According to the Marxists, 'the people' does not mean the nation but the proletariat, the term used to describe the increasingly numerous lower or working classes who are paid a wage, but do not reap the real profits from their labour. In the Marxist's utopian vision, the overthrow of the nobility during the French Revolution was necessary, but it was only the first step in the liberation of the people. Another, proletarian revolution would follow, which would in its turn overthrow the bourgeoisie and give real power to the working man, who would no longer be exploited by capitalist owners. This would be the final revolution, which would result for the first time in a classless society, based on common ownership of property and real economic and social equality for all.

In order to achieve the proletarian revolution, Marxist thinkers needed first to educate the masses, to convince them that victory was possible and to secure their loyalty and support for the future battle. It was with this goal in mind that Karl Marx wrote *The communist manifesto* in 1848, an excerpt from which appears at the end of this chapter (see Document 5.1). Marx goes into some detail in explaining the historical reasons behind class development, the economic situation of the proletariat in the mid-nineteenth century and the ways in which the workers are exploited by the bourgeoisie, and he suggests a solution in the form of the communist or proletarian revolution. He also explains the relationship of the proletariat and the coming revolution to the existing political structure of nations.

Since one of the achievements of the nations in the nineteenth century was to consolidate and centralise their economies, the logical first step in the proletarian revolution is for the workers to act within the existing structure of their nations to develop co-ordinated action against their middle-class oppressors. This did not mean, however, that the proletarian struggle was essentially a national one. On the contrary, what defined the solidarity of workers was their class, not their nation, and Marx claimed that for the proletarian revolution to succeed it needed to be international in scope. The role of the communists, he asserted, was to co-ordinate the activities of the workers of the different countries, pointing out to them how their struggles were the same, independent of nationality, and eventually to unite the whole of the proletariat.

Once the workers had begun to organise themselves nationally, the time would come for the movement as a whole to unite and overthrow the bourgeoisie all at once, casting aside the artificial and bourgeois notion of nationality. Workers do not have a country, argued Marx, but are tied to the other workers of all places in a universal class bond. This brings back the idea that 'the people' means the workers, not the nation, and once again demonstrates the fundamental opposition between class theory and the idea of the nation. Marxists argue that the nation is an artificial construction designed to make the workers forget their true links with the other members of their class, and to divide the workers one against the other in order to preserve bourgeois domination. For Marx, a truly emancipated proletariat is one which has eliminated national rivalries and concentrates on the inevitable revolution which will bring about the classless society. This is most clearly expressed in the famous invocation at the end of *The communist manifesto*: 'Working men of all countries, unite!'

With these arguments and promises, Marx and his colleagues hoped to unite the workers of the international proletariat in one great movement. In order to do so they were competing against the arguments of the nationalists, who were also seeking to win the loyalty and support of the masses. As we have seen in the preceding two chapters, the national arguments were strong and also had great sentimental appeal. While both movements attracted supporters, several factors were in the end working in favour of the nation over class.

The two ideologies in conflict

First of all, while the workers of all countries may have all belonged to one class in theory, and thus had in common the economic conditions of their class, in practice they were an extremely heterogeneous group. In addition to the obvious cultural differences such as language and religion, the diversity of the kinds of work they undertook was so great that it was often understandably difficult for the workers themselves to recognise or feel the common bonds which the Marxists claimed held them together. The different conditions of employment from one region to another, and from one industry to another, the varying skill levels required for different jobs and the resulting inequality in levels of pay and living conditions meant, for example, that the skilled mine worker did not readily identify himself with the unskilled day labourer. Thus even in the area that supposedly united the workers – economic conditions – the reality was that there were significant inequalities between different sub-groups according to the particular industry or local conditions.

The great diversity that characterised the working classes actually acted as a barrier to class solidarity, and made the goal of international unity and working-class consciousness more difficult to realise. The internationalist doctrine did have greater appeal in some urban areas which attracted large numbers of immigrants from diverse regions, resulting in a mixed population. In such cities as Vienna, which boasted a large cultural and ethnic mixture among its workers, the arguments in favour of international class solidarity and similarity of situation seemed relatively acceptable, since they corresponded with the workers' experience; they knew and could see around them workers of other nationalities in the same plight as themselves. This kind of urban situation was exceptional in the context of the whole of Europe, however. The majority of workers in the smaller or less international agglomerations could not easily identify with other workers, who were culturally distinct from themselves and lived and worked in completely different conditions. The idea of the international proletariat and working-class solidarity, therefore, was less immediately appealing to many workers as a basis for group consciousness than the idea of the nation, since what the workers had in common was not always obvious.

The internationalist aspect of the Marxist analysis was also hindered by the national form which some of the working-class movements began to take. For example, one of the first claims of workers in Europe was the right to vote. This particular fight did help to unify all of the workers who were not wealthy enough to qualify for the franchise, and contributed to an increase in class-based political consciousness. At the same time, however, participation in politics was always national, by definition. Even if some workers began to think in terms of class solidarity, if the goal was for national political rights the struggle increased their national consciousness and was in no way bringing them closer to the kind of international solidarity which the Marxists considered necessary. Thus the first steps towards proletarian liberation, in which the workers of each country dealt with their own national bourgeoisie, were actually counter-productive to the second, the international proletarian revolution. As workers began to develop class consciousness through their national organisations, they were at the same time strengthening their national identity. Thus the national workers' organisations could in part themselves undermine the idea of class-based international proletarian solidarity aimed at eliminating the 'bourgeois' nations.

This is not to say that the Marxist doctrines of working-class solidarity and opposition to bourgeois interests did not have any success in Europe during the nineteenth and twentieth centuries, only that the strictly *internationalist* dimension of the doctrine was unable to rival nationalism. Workers did feel solidarity with other workers, but mostly with workers of the same nationality. Part of the explanation for the strength of nationalism lies in the fact that national identity and national loyalty were not held to be incompatible with other identities and loyalties. For the nationalists, no contradiction necessarily exists between being, say, German and being a worker (or a doctor or whatever). According to strict Marxist orthodoxy, however, being a worker was the primary, fundamental, even unique determining criterion of identity for all members of the proletariat. Workers did not belong to any nation; in other words, they had no nationality. The kinds of duties implied by national loyalties were in fact tricks to get workers to submit to bourgeois power. In this way, a strict or literal interpretation of Marx's works revealed that his ideology was diametrically opposed to nationalism, to the extent that nationalism and Marxism were incompatible. The restricted, international perspective of Marxism was gradually marginalised among the different national working-class movements, while other aspects of Marx's doctrine were retained and adapted to fit the needs of particular local or national circumstances.

The conflict between the ideologies of nationalism and Marxism grew much sharper towards the end of the nineteenth century in the Europe of nation-states. Although *The communist manifesto* was written in 1848, and the principal strains of the ideology of class were formed during the first part of the century, the class-oriented movement itself was still only in the organising or early phases of development at that time. Also, until then the two strains of thought were partly united through their common opposition to absolutism. The revolutions of 1848, for example, were held by both nationalists and Marxists to indicate the growing relevance of their claims and the truth of their analyses. Once absolutism was defeated (in western Europe) and the nation-state came to be the dominant form of political organisation, the differences between the two progressive ideologies were more sharply articulated, and the class-based movements began to become more organised and to grow in strength.

Several types of working-class movement appeared. These can be generalised into two forms: trade-union movements, and working-class or socialist political parties. Each drew upon some elements of the Marxist doctrine. They were usually organised at first along national lines, meeting occasionally at international working-men's conferences to attempt to bring about the unity of the entire proletariat which Karl Marx had hoped for. The international, or perhaps anti-national, position was upheld by some of the members, but the movements were so diverse that agreement on strategies was difficult for them to achieve. Certainly not everyone supported that position. From the outset, disagreement reigned over the very appropriateness of the working-class political parties in the first place. Some believed that they could only help the working man's situation, while others felt that they were merely a distraction from the real preparation for the revolution, and were actually a disadvantage to the proletariat as a whole.

On a smaller scale, the various trade unions were often more concerned with the particular situation of the workers they represented than with the condition of workers in general, and the socialist parties were most often limited by their national political situations. For example, in most of the western European countries the socialist parties were fighting, among other things, for universal suffrage. In France, however, that had already been achieved, and so French delegates to the international meetings were supportive of, but not fundamentally interested in, that item of the agenda. From the latter half of the nineteenth century onwards, delegates representing countries from all over Europe met together as the Workers International, in an effort to increase international co-operation among socialists and trade unionists and to further the aims of the proletariat. While some of the socialist and trade-union movements had success in their own countries, as a whole the International was unsuccessful in its goal of a world-wide revolution of the working class.

Thus, history has seen the partial modification of Marx's ideas and the impact of Marxism on the social, political and economic development of Europe, but not by bringing about international worker solidarity and the end of the bourgeois nations through a world-wide revolution. Marxist-inspired revolutions, where they occurred, always took place within the context of a particular nation. But what concerns us here about the class movements is principally how this new challenge was met by nations and nationalists, and in what ways national doctrine was affected and transformed by the threatening rise of these – if not in practice, then at least in declaration – avowedly international progressive movements.

This chapter has not attempted a historical or a sociological analysis of the Marxist concept of social class, which would demonstrate that class is as much an 'imagined community' as the nation. The goal here has been to place European nationalism in perspective by presenting another interpretation of European history since the French Revolution based not upon the nation, but upon the idea of social class. It has also been to show that the existence of these two competing interpretations has implications not only for our retrospective historical understanding, but also for the choices made by the political actors of the period and the ways in which the ideologies themselves evolved. In particular, the emergence of a Marxist ideology on the left modified the significance and the development of nationalism from the second half of the nineteenth century onwards.

Around 1870, liberal nationalism lost its status as 'idealistic', revolutionary and avant-garde as it became the established ideology of the ruling classes. It was challenged at this time by the ideology of class, which declared itself to be more progressive than bourgeois nationalism. Faced with this Marxist criticism now that it found itself in the dominant position, nationalism became trans-formed into something more conservative than it had been when it opposed absolutism throughout the first part of the nineteenth century. The primary reaction was to increase the pursuit of popular support and loyalty to the nation and national institutions through the emotional nationalist arguments and policies we have examined in the preceding two chapters. At the same time, in response to the limited, but not insignificant, electoral successes of some of the socialist parties, social reform was slowly achieved in parts of western Europe. In the next chapter we shall be looking at how nationalism and the politics of nation-states developed and adapted during the years from 1870 until the First World War, the period of popular nationalism.

An alternative to nationalism

5.1 Excerpt from *The communist manifesto* by Karl Marx

The history of all hitherto existing society is the history of class struggles.

Freeman and slave, patrician and plebeian, lord and serf, guild/master and journeyman – in a word, oppressor and oppressed, stood in constant opposition to one another, carried on an uninterrupted, now hidden, now open fight, a fight that each time ended either in a revolutionary re-constitution of society at large or in the common ruin of the contending classes.

In the earlier epochs of history, we find almost everywhere a complicated arrangement of society into various orders, a manifold gradation of social rank . . .

The modern bourgeois society that has sprouted from the ruins of feudal society has not done away with class antagonisms. It has but established new classes, new conditions of oppression, new forms of struggle in place of the old ones.

Our epoch, the epoch of the bourgeoisie, possesses, however, this distinctive feature: it has simplified the class antagonisms. Society as a whole is more and more splitting into two great hostile camps, into two great classes directly facing one another: Bourgeoisie and Proletariat . . .

The bourgeoisie has, through its exploitation of the world market, given a cosmopolitan character to production and consumption in every country. To the great chagrin of Reactionists, it has drawn from under the feet of industry the national ground on which it stood. All old-established national industries have been destroyed or are daily being destroyed. They are dislodged by new industries, whose introduction becomes a life-and-death question for all civilised nations, by industries that no longer work up indigenous raw material, but raw material drawn from the remotest zones; industries whose products are consumed, not only at home, but in every quarter of the globe. In place of the old wants, satisfied by the productions of the country, we now find wants, requiring for their satisfaction the products of distant lands and climes. In place of the old local and national seclusion and self-sufficiency, we have intercourse in every direction, universal interdependence of nations. And as in material, so also in intellectual production. The intellectual creations of individual nations become common property. National one-sidedness and narrow-mindedness become more and more impossible, and from the numerous national and local literatures, there arises a world literature.

The bourgeoisie, by the rapid improvement of all instruments of production, by the immensely facilitated means of communication, draws all, even the most barbarian, nations into civilisation. The cheap prices of its commodities are the heavy artillery with which it batters down the Chinese walls, with which it forces the barbarians' intensely obstinate hatred of foreigners to capitulate. It compels all nations, on pain of extinction, to adopt the bourgeois mode of production; it compels them to introduce what it calls civilisation into their midst, i.e., to become bourgeois themselves. In one word, it creates a world after its own image.

The bourgeoisie has subjected the country to the rule of the towns. It has created enormous cities, has greatly increased the urban population as compared with the rural, and has thus rescued a considerable part of the population from the idiocy of rural life. Just as it has made the country dependent on the towns, so it has made the barbarian and semi-barbarian countries dependent on the civilised ones, nations of peasants on nations of bourgeois, the East on the West.

The bourgeoisie keeps more and more doing away with the scattered state of the population, of the means of production, and of property. It has agglomerated population, centralised means of production, and has concentrated property in a few hands. The necessary consequence of this was political centralisation. Independent but loosely connected provinces, with separate interests, laws, governments, and systems of taxation, became lumped together into one nation, with one government, one code of laws, one national class-interest, one frontier and one customs-tariff . . .

Though not in substance, yet in form, the struggle of the proletariat with the bourgeoisie is at first a national struggle. The proletariat of each country must, of course, first of all settle matters with its own bourgeoisie . . .

Class versus nation

In what relation do the Communists stand to the proletarians as a whole? . . . The Communists are distinguished from other working-class parties by this only: 1. In the national struggles of the proletarians of the different countries, they point out and bring to the front the common interests of the entire proletariat, independently of all nationality. 2. In the various stages of development which the struggle of the working class against the bourgeoisie has to pass through, they always and everywhere represent the interests of the movement as a whole . . .

The Communists are . . . reproached with desiring to abolish countries and nationality.

The working men have no country. We cannot take from them what they have not got. Since the proletariat must first of all acquire political supremacy, must rise to be the leading class of the nation, must constitute itself *the* nation, it is, so far, itself national, though not in the bourgeois sense of the word.

National differences and antagonisms between peoples are daily more and more vanishing, owing to the development of the bourgeoisie, to freedom of commerce, to the world-market, to uniformity in the mode of production and the conditions of life corresponding thereto.

The supremacy of the proletariat will cause them to vanish still faster. United action, of the leading civilised countries at least, is one of the first conditions for the emancipation of the proletariat.

In proportion as the exploitation of one individual by another is put an end to, the exploitation of one nation by another will also be put an end to. In proportion as the antagonism between classes within the nation vanishes, the hostility of one nation to another will come to an end . . .

In short, the Communists everywhere support every revolutionary movement against the existing social and political order of things . . .

Finally, they labour everywhere for the union and agreement of the democratic parties of all countries.

The Communists disdain to conceal their views and aims. They openly declare that their ends can be attained only by the forcible overthrow of all existing social conditions. Let the ruling classes tremble at a Communistic revolution. The proletarians have nothing to lose but their chains. They have a world to win.

WORKING MEN OF ALL COUNTRIES, UNITE!

Source: K. Marx, 'The communist manifesto', in D. McLellan (ed.), *Karl Marx: selected writings*, Oxford, 1977 [1848]

Document case-study questions

1 Why do working men have no countries?

2 What is the role of the nation in Marx's analysis of society?

3 How and why does Marx see national differences disappearing?

Nationalism's popular phase, 1870–1914

Once the liberal nationalism of the early nineteenth century had achieved its major objectives and become the official doctrine of nation-states, it could no longer be the fundamental element of the ideology of reform. Quite the opposite, as we have seen in the previous chapter; social and political reformers in later nineteenth-century Europe were more attracted by the socialist and trade-unionist movements influenced by Marx, and took up a non-national or even anti-national stand. No longer a 'progressive' ideology, nationalism was nevertheless a powerful influence over the vast majority of European people in the 40 years leading up to the First World War, a period in which the masses gained national identities. In achieving this ideological dominance, nationalism was defended and promulgated by two different groups: the governments of the nation-states themselves, and elements of the conservative right. In each case, the idea of the nation and nationalism was transformed in order to meet the needs of the group that was promoting it.

State nationalism

The governments of nation-states, in order to make the defence of the nation and the indoctrination of the people become official state policy, refined their own particular national identity and mythology and set out to propagate those amongst the population. No longer restricted to an educated elite, the national-ism of the state was based less upon the legalistic concepts coming from the French Revolution, and was instead tied to emotional arguments and to the emphasis on particular national traits that came to be central in the popular-isation of a state's national identity. Chapters 3 and 4 described the different kinds of national definitions and the ways in which states used various characteristics to form their own, seemingly unique identity. The goal was to create a sense of loyalty and unity among their citizens, as well as a cultural homogeneity capable of reducing the risk of socio-economic (class-based) conflicts. With the resources of the states behind them, government nationalists were indeed successful in popularising the idea of the nation, and in integrating (at least partly) the masses of their populations into their various nations.

Germany

In the newly united Germany, the years 1871–90 were called the *Gründerjahre* or grounding years and in spite of the economic success of the united Reich, the government had to deal with the problem of unity. Bismarck implemented a policy of relative centralisation, although certain states – such as Bavaria, Saxony and Württemberg – retained their independent armies and postal services, and some regional culture was maintained. Universal male suffrage, which began in 1867, was an important factor in eliminating local particularisms since it encouraged the formation of national political parties. German public primary schools, among the earliest in Europe, were able to promote the German language effectively throughout the country. The *Kulturkampf*, as we saw briefly in Chapter 4, was Bismarck's policy aimed at weakening the Roman Catholic church, the social democrats and the regions as political forces. A combined policy of colonisation and oppressive laws prohibiting the use of minority languages was aimed at the Danish, Polish and Alsatian minorities, in an effort to integrate them into the nation. After the fall of Bismarck in 1890, these national integration policies were increased in intensity. The three minorities just mentioned had only been partly integrated by the time the regions in which they lived had been taken away from Germany following the First World War. Notwithstanding these exceptions, the German policy of national integration was on the whole a success, and the populations of the Reich experienced a strong sentiment of loyalty and patriotism to their nation.

Italy

In Italy, the situation differed slightly from that in Germany. The overall economic fragility of the nation, which comprised an industrialising north and an agricultural south, led to a similarly fragile social structure that put national cohesion in jeopardy. Lower general literacy rates and a more backward school system made the schools less effective at teaching Italian to the masses than schools in Germany were at teaching German. Politically, suffrage was limited at first to 2 per cent of the population, weakening the popular legitimacy of the nation, and did not become universal (for males) until 1912. Because of the lack of help from national political parties seeking popular mandates in the earlier years, it took a longer time for the idea of the nation to penetrate the countryside. For these reasons, national unity in Italy was more fragile than in Germany and France.

Russia

In Russia, the tsarist regime also sought to follow the nationalist model and instigate cultural unity among its people. A programme of Russification combined with an attempt to impose Russian Orthodoxy was instigated throughout the realm. Meeting with some success, this move was resisted strongly, however, by the various other churches – the Roman Catholic church in Polish Russia, the Ukrainian Orthodox church in the Ukraine, and the Lutheran churches in the Baltic states. Each of these churches formed a core around which a sense of nationalist opposition to Russia was able to develop. Growing national consciousness among the populations of Russia was very much linked to religious adherence, as was also the case in Roman Catholic Ireland within the mainly Protestant United Kingdom.

Emerging nations

Nationalism was also entering a popular phase in the would-be nations that did not have a state of their own during this period, such as among the diverse peoples of the Austro-Hungarian and Russian Empires, and in Ireland. This was achieved partly through the aid of the non-state churches, as we have seen. Also instrumental was the development of a network of specific-interest organisations run by nationalists hoping to gain in autonomy at the expense of the state; these spread their causes locally in areas where the larger state had a reduced institutional presence. In Ireland, such groups as the Land and Labour Association, the Gaelic Athletic Association and the United Irish League gradually encouraged Irish national consciousness and mobilised local support for the issue of Irish independence. Among the 'nations' in the Austro-Hungarian Empire, the securing of official status for the teaching of their languages was a significant step towards the development of national consciousness.

In the case of both Austria-Hungary and Ireland, the growth of democracy provided a further vehicle for the expression of the growing national conscious-ness. Building on the local support and awareness achieved through the many small organisations, the Irish sent nationalist representatives to the British parliament who, with their collective impact, were able to bring the Irish national question to the forefront. In the Austro-Hungarian Empire, the division between the blocs of representatives who were first and foremost nationalists actually blocked the functioning of the assembly by preventing any majority from forming, and each group demanded the kind of legislative autonomy the Hungarians had achieved in 1867. Thus whether we are looking at the existing nation-states or sub-state national groups with some measure of official recognition, national consciousness was increasing among the peoples of Europe.

Right-wing nationalism

The spread of cultural and ethnic popular nationalism from the official policy of the nation-states was further reinforced and even amplified by the second type of nationalism to develop towards the end of the nineteenth century, that of the conservative right. Preoccupied with maintaining order, the right in several countries saw the strengthening of the nation as a way to preserve the existing social hierarchy. These groups emphasised exclusively the emotional side of the ideology of nationalism, encouraging patriotism and the belief that the nation could do no wrong, and denouncing as traitors to the state and nation any who disagreed with them. They used nationalism as a weapon against anti-national socialist or Marxist left-wing movements, which they considered to be a threat to the existing order. They also used nationalism to increase support for the military, a traditional bastion of order and the right, in the name of the defence of the glory and prestige of the nation against all rivals. Characteristic of this new form of nationalism – and never before associated with nationalism – were outright distrust of foreigners, racism and anti-semitism. It was at this time that the term 'nationalism' was first employed, to describe these right-wing movements whose overt flag-waving and aggressively hostile patriotism were becoming increasingly visible.

France

This type of nationalism was characterised in France by the movement known as the *Action Française*. Founded in 1899, its ideas were spread by its polemic, controversial and extremely aggressive newspaper of the same name. The members of the *Action Française*, especially its leader Charles Maurras, brought together a kind of integral nationalism according to which no political value could be held more important than national greatness, with monarchism representing the best system of ensuring that greatness. The members committed themselves to combating the republic in the name of the nation. While they attracted few converts to monarchism, the force of their nationalism set the tone for the whole of France, and propelled other political groups into taking more aggressive, nationalistic stances.

Italy

A similar nationalist movement developed in Italy as it struggled through a social and political crisis at the end of the nineteenth century. These nationalists did not hesitate to criticise the failure of the Italian government to achieve greater national unity among the regions. Led by Enrico Corradini, they drew upon the legend of the greatness of ancient Rome in calling for a violent response to what they labelled the anti-national forces weakening Italy. These nationalists were the antecedents of fascism, which would come to power in Italy in the 1920s.

Austria

In Austria, the extreme nationalists did not hide their aversion for the minority peoples of the empire and their sympathy for pan-Germanism. They considered violence to be a perfectly legitimate political weapon. Such leaders as Georg Schönerer sought popular support for their anti-semitic, anti-minority, anti-parliamentary position, and criticised the empire's pragmatic approach to the nationality problem.

This new type of nationalism characteristic of the conservative right was strengthened by the support of an increasing number of artists and intellectuals from across the political spectrum. Disappointed by declining moral standards, a society preoccupied with materialism and the cruelty of the industrial system, they turned the nation into a righteous principle that could rejuvenate their society. They valued the spirit of individual sacrifice for the good of the nation. Many had been revolutionaries in their youth, and only later became supporters of conservative nationalist ideas. In Germany, Richard Wagner's *Ring cycle*; in France, Maurice Barrès' *Les Déracinés*; and in Russia, Fyodor Dostoevsky's *The possessed* all strongly praise the spiritual richness of their respective national traditions and cultures. The last two also criticise any theory that claims to be universal – such as Marxism or the Rights of Man – and which is not strongly grounded in a national cultural tradition. These artists and writers contributed to the growing strength of national mythologies, turning customs into cultural values, and making the nation into something sacred and holy, something spiritual.

The age of conservative nationalism

Looking back over the period we have covered so far, we see that the idea of the nation popularised by the governments in the late nineteenth century differed in several ways from the one that had been in the ascendant during the revolutionary and reforming periods earlier in the century. The state nationalists abandoned in practice the belief that popular will was necessary for the formation of nations – although some, such as Renan, continued to discuss it in theory. The idea that individuals could decide to form a nation, that the very fact of deciding would make them one, and that their willingness was a requirement for forming a nation (Chapter 3 covers this in more detail) was quickly discarded or minimalised by authorities anxious to prevent any other groups from setting themselves up as rivals to their official position. They preferred to emphasise culture and race, inflexible in definition and impossible to change, which would not permit regions simply to 'decide' that they were a different nation and attempt to break away. A region belonged to a race or even a culture, and that was that. National sentiments were encouraged within existing nation-states or existing groups that had secured some form of official recognition for their culture community, but they were not encouraged with respect to just any group that fancied itself a nation.

Economy and society

The changing economic and social conditions at the end of the nineteenth century led to the downplaying of the kind of liberalism associated with nationalism in its earlier phase.

Those countries that sought to keep up with the pace of industrialisation often found policies of national protectionism a more appealing and promising route than economic liberalism. Protectionism was easily compatible with the new style of nationalism; it stressed favouring the nation and protecting it from 'foreign' competition. The migration of peoples to industrial centres also contributed to feelings of 'national' resentment that foreigners could come and take the better jobs (whether this was actually happening or not). Such rivalry was also present among the middle classes in the multi-national states such as Austria-Hungary, where much of the nationalist agitation was over competition for local minor official positions (such as postmaster), which had to be decided by the languages spoken and written by the candidates in question.

The economic depression of the end of the century (1873–95) accentuated the calls to find national solutions and to reinforce borders and develop the national economies through, for example, national transportation and communication networks. These economic and social changes provided governments and nationalists with numerous opportunities to promote their own exclusivist policies and ideas by asserting hostility towards foreigners, and playing upon emotional nationalism.

The Dreyfus Affair

The difference between the nationalism of the revolution and that of the end of the century is illustrated by the social and political crisis in France brought about by the Dreyfus Affair at the end of the century. A French army officer, Alfred Dreyfus, was mistakenly accused of handing over French military secrets to Germany, largely because he was Jewish. When the army refused to go back on its original guilty verdict in spite of evidence to the contrary, the situation blew up into a major political scandal which divided French society down the middle. The majority supported the 'nationalist' stance. This asserted that Dreyfus, being Jewish and therefore a foreigner, was probably guilty of treason anyway; and that the most important element in his conviction was the safeguarding of order and preservation of the prestige and honour of the national military, even if that meant that this one man was treated unjustly. Several of the nationalist intellectuals and politicians formed a group called the League for the French *Patrie* whose views embodied an intimate connection between nationalism and anti-semitic racism. They formed the opposite camp to the League of the Rights of Man, who wanted Dreyfus retried and pronounced innocent (which he was). These opposing attitudes reveal the full circle that nationalism had made in France, from defending the idea of the rights of man in 1789 to opposing that same idea in 1898 – in the name of defence of the nation and of its prestige.

National humiliation

A further characteristic of the nationalism of the period 1870–1914 is its link with perceived national humiliation. If the country felt humiliated in any way, this became a theme which nationalists could develop, attempting to focus the attention of the masses on solutions, which were always linked to a strengthening of national cultural purity and aimed at reducing foreign influence. For example, Italy was humiliated by its weak economy and its failure to achieve better results from national unity, as well as by the fact that some 'Italians' were still ruled by Austria and the Italian state was too weak to reclaim them. In France, it was military defeat at the hands of Prussia in 1870–71 and the subsequent loss of the French provinces of Alsace and Lorraine that was loudly talked about, and the sentiment of revenge fuelled the growing nationalism of the right. In eastern Europe, the minority groups in the Austro-Hungarian and Russian Empires developed a sense of cultural humiliation, playing up slights to minor officials who were not expert in the 'higher' language. Nationalism bred of perceived humiliation tended to be extremely violent in its rhetoric and its demands for concrete responses on the part of political leaders. Great Britain, which did not suffer from this kind of humiliation, was less susceptible to extreme revengeful nationalism. Nationalism bred of pride in success and empire, although important, was of a less violent nature, as we shall see in the next chapter.

Democracy

In the final quarter of the nineteenth century, nationalism grew to become one of the most potent forces in European society and politics. More and more countries expanded their democratic base, increasing dramatically the numbers of males with the vote. Through their participation in politics, the population as a whole became more than ever aware of the larger world beyond their immediate reach, and of their place in society. Once given political influence, albeit small, the people were courted by many groups seeking their favour and support, and campaigns were waged to 'educate' the population, and to teach the people who they were and what their political role ought to be. Nationalism, taught by the state and favoured by circumstances, had a notable ability to motivate populations through its tremendous emotional appeal. Democracy pushed European leaders to try harder to integrate the mass of their people in order to avoid social disruption and maintain a certain order in society. The cultivation of loyalty through attachment to national values and the development of national identity was a crucial means to achieve this end.

Popular nationalism

At the same time as it was becoming a significant political force and gaining an influence over larger numbers of people, the nationalism of the period 1870–1914 demonstrated several characteristics that distinguished it from the nationalism of the earlier period. No longer quite as uniform across Europe, nationalism began to take on different forms which depended more closely upon local conditions. National models or identities could be based on different kinds of characteristics and articulated by nationalists in different ways, depending upon the circum-stances. As we have seen over the past few chapters, no single model of national identity can be found. The sociologist Max Weber attempted to identify the common element among the diversity of ways to define the nation, and ended up by concluding that the similarity, however differently the national communities were defined, lay in the goal of forming a separate, autonomous political entity (see Document 6.1). Even if, as in several nations within the Austro-Hungarian Empire, they were at first content with official recognition of their language and limited political representation, as national identity developed and intensified, the nationalists would – according to Weber – not be satisfied with anything less than a state of their own on the western European model. The fact that they aimed to build, unite or reinforce the same kind of political entity, a state, was by the end of the nineteenth century the only common point within the diverse forms of nationalism.

In addition to the diversity of forms of national identity, as we have seen, the official state policy of assimilation in western Europe and that of recognised groups seeking to develop national cultures differed in aim and style from the aggressive patriotic nationalism of the conservative right vying for influence within the existing nation-states. Thus a variety of ways to conceive nations were developed, with each nation described by its proponents in greater and greater detail in order to refine the national image and have it accepted by the members of the nation.

The new forms of nationalism which appeared at the end of the nineteenth century no longer defined their national political entities through a legal principle stressing popular will, but by a common race or culture. The popular nationalism of this period emphasised the emotional attachment to a perceived ethnically and culturally homogeneous group, defining itself in opposition to 'others'. Supported by some of the leading scientific theories of the day, the essential opposition between nations and their definition in ethnic terms led occasionally to downright racism on the part of nationalists. Nationalists in those instances not only denounced foreigners as the enemies of the nation who stood in the way of the nation's attaining its rightful place and the glory that was its due, but sometimes went so far as to preach the superiority of their race among their followers.

The nationalism of the popular phase was a nationalism of competition between nations: competition to stake out a claim for their national territory and – for those not already a state – to form a separate state in which to achieve national unity, integrate the population into the national culture, and teach the people to be patriotic and believe in the greatness and superiority of their nation. The competition between nations included a race for economic and industrial development, for military success, and for cultural achievement – demonstrating that their national culture could provide the world's best music, writing, painting and so on.

The competition spread outside Europe to the rest of the world, in the form of seeking to colonise and dominate the largest territory, to build a vaster empire than the other nations. The next chapter will be devoted to an analysis of the relationship between nationalism and the imperialism characteristic of the period.

Document case study

A sociological study of nationalism

6.1 Excerpt from 'The nation' by Max Weber

If the concept of 'nation' can in any way be defined unambiguously, it certainly cannot be stated in terms of empirical qualities common to those who count as members of the nation. In the sense of those using the term at a given time, the concept undoubtedly means, above all, that one may exact from certain groups of men a specific sentiment of solidarity in the face of other groups. Thus, the concept belongs in the sphere of values. Yet, there is no agreement on how these groups should be delimited or about what concerted action should result from such solidarity.

In ordinary language, 'nation' is, first of all, not identical with the 'people of a state,' that is, with the membership of a given polity. Numerous polities comprise groups among whom the independence of their 'nation' is emphatically asserted in the face of the other groups; or, on the other hand, they comprise parts of a group whose members declare this group to be one homogeneous 'nation' (Austria before 1918, for example). Furthermore, a 'nation' is not identical with a community speaking the same language; that this by no means suffices is indicated by the Serbs and Croats, the North Americans, the Irish, and the English. On the contrary, a common language does not seem to be absolutely necessary to a 'nation'. In official documents, besides 'Swiss people' one also finds the phrase 'Swiss Nation'. And some language groups do not think of themselves as a separate 'nation,' for example, at least until recently, the white Russians. The pretension, however, to be considered a special 'nation' is regularly associated with a common language as a culture value of the masses; this is predominantly the case in the classic country of language conflicts, Austria, and equally so in Russia and in eastern Prussia. But this linkage of the common language and 'nation' is of varying intensity; for instance, it is very low in the United States as well as in Canada.

'National' solidarity among men speaking the same language may be just as well rejected as accepted. Solidarity, instead, may be linked with differences in the other great 'culture value of the masses,' namely, a religious creed, as is the case with the Serbs and the Croats. National solidarity may be connected with differing social structure and mores and hence with 'ethnic' elements, as is the case with the German Swiss and the Alsatians in the face of the Germans of the Reich, or with the Irish facing the British. Yet above all, national solidarity may be linked to memories of a common political destiny with other nations, among the Alsatians with the French since the revolutionary war which represents their common heroic age, just as among the Baltic Barons with the Russians whose political destiny they helped to steer.

It goes without saying that 'national' affiliation need not be based upon common blood. Indeed, everywhere the especially radical 'nationalists' are often of foreign descent . . . Nevertheless, the idea of the 'nation' is apt to include the notions of common descent and of an essential, though frequently indefinite, homogeneity. The nation has these notions in common with the sentiment of solidarity of ethnic communities, which is also nourished from various sources. But the sentiment of ethnic solidarity does not by itself make a 'nation' . . . The Poles of Upper Silesia, until recently, had hardly any feeling of solidarity with the 'Polish Nation'. They felt themselves to be a separate ethnic group in the face of the Germans, but for the rest they were Prussian subjects and nothing else. . . .

There are, on the other hand, social groups that profess indifference to, and even directly relinquish, an evaluational adherence to a single nation. At the present time, certain leading strata of the class movement of the modern proletariat consider such indifference and relinquishment to be an accomplishment. Their argument meets with varying success, depending upon political and linguistic affiliations and also upon different strata to the proletariat; on the whole, their success is rather diminishing at the present time.

. . .

In so far as there is at all a common object lying behind the obviously ambiguous term 'nation,' it is apparently located in the field of politics. One might well define the concept of nation in the following way: a nation is a community of sentiment which would adequately manifest itself in a state of its own; hence, a nation is a community which normally tends to produce a state of its own.

The causal components that lead to the emergence of a national sentiment in this sense may vary greatly. If we for once disregard religious belief – which has not yet played its last role in this matter, especially among the Serbs and the Croats – then common, purely political destinies have first to be considered. Under certain conditions, otherwise heterogeneous peoples can be melted together through common destinies. The reason for the Alsatians' not feeling themselves as belonging to the German nation has to be sought in memories. Their political destiny has taken its course outside the German sphere for too long; their heroes are the heroes of French history . . .

An existing state organisation whose heroic age is not felt as such by the masses can nevertheless be decisive for a powerful sentiment of solidarity, in spite of the greatest internal antagonism. The state is valued as the agency that guarantees security, and this is above all the case in times of external danger, when sentiments of national solidarity flare up . . .

If one believes that it is at all expedient to distinguish national sentiment as something homogeneous and specifically set apart, one can do so only by referring to a tendency towards an autonomous state. And one must clearly be aware of the fact that sentiments of solidarity, very heterogeneous in both their nature and their origin, are comprised within national sentiments.

Source: H. H. Gerth and C. Wright Mills (eds. and trans.), *From Max Weber: essays in sociology*, **London, 1948**

Document case-study questions

1 How does Document 6.1 reject the 'objective' qualities often attributed to nations?

2 Why does Document 6.1 define a nation as a community which normally tends to produce a state of its own?

3 How does the definition of a nation in Document 6.1 compare with that of Document 4.1?

7 Imperialism and nationalism

For several centuries most of the European powers had been engaged in overseas exploration, trade, conquest and colonisation. During the nineteenth century, however, the area of the globe that came under direct European influence increased at an unprecedented rate as the European nations sought to increase their predominance in world affairs. 'Imperialism' is the term which has been given to this European expansion, this direct control and subjugation of other areas of the world to European domination. Imperialism has been the object of many studies, and numerous theories have been expressed about the motivation behind the European desire for expansion and ultimate success in conquering most of the world. These explanations include the desire for increased profits to be made by expanding markets and finding cheaper raw materials abroad; the belief that it was the duty of the civilised world to bring civilisation and modernity to the backward peoples and regions of the globe, along with Christianity; and not least the nationalist desire for glory and prestige which colonies brought to the mother country.

This chapter will first of all examine the extent to which nationalism and the competition between nations contributed to the drive towards imperial expansion. A serious debate over the relative importance of the causes of imperialism has been going on since the imperial period. This is not the place to resolve the conflict, but it is worth considering the part that nationalism has been credited with playing, in order to appreciate the significance of the phenomenon of nationalism. Secondly, irrespective of whether it was a cause of imperial expansion, the drive for colonies could not but affect the European nations; and it will also be worth while to consider the influence imperialism had on the nations themselves, on their identities and on nationalist ideology.

National competition

The imperial expansion of the nineteenth century can to some extent be considered a mere extension of the competition between nations – the desire to demonstrate that one's own nation was the best and would show the way for the rest of the world. In the popular phase of nationalism, when the nation was defined in a large part in opposition to other nations, and in which national rivalries intensified, the acquisition of an overseas empire came to be seen as a necessity for demonstrating national grandeur. The pursuit of colonies was also held to be essential in the industrialising world in order to keep up and expand economically, and it provided a good way of gaining the military success that was required of any nation which wanted to call itself great. Many leaders were keen to bring glory to their nation. At the same time they used imperialism as a way of solidifying support for the nation and focusing on tensions away from home rather than on internal ones. Colonies could also contribute to the fulfilment of the need to bring civilisation to the world, a missionary spirit which came with the belief in modernity and progress. The growing sense of national identity meant that for many European nations the civilisation they were exporting was essentially a national one. Thus while the purely economic and military arguments leading to imperialism are strong, the fact that European nation-states embarked on vast projects of imperial expansion was at least in part linked to their increasing sense of nationalism, their desire to bring glory to their nation, and their rivalry and competition with other nations.

Great Britain

The case of Great Britain differs slightly from the other examples of imperial expansion in the nineteenth century. Britain already possessed a large quantity of territory by the first half of the nineteenth century. Having built upon the work of previous centuries, and having the advantage of a dominant position at the treaty of Vienna in 1815, it was able to develop what would become the largest of the European empires. With strategic colonies in all parts of the world, and possessing the largest naval force in the world, Britain ruled the seas and dominated global politics throughout the nineteenth century. For the most part, the British Empire pre-dates the period of the development of nationalism, which cannot therefore be held to be a principal cause of British imperial expansion, as was the case with some of the other European nations.

While nationalism may not have contributed originally to British imperialism, the British sense of pride and national greatness after 1870 was unquestionably linked to its imperial success, and the British sense of nation and national identity was even more closely associated with its overseas empire than was that of any of the other European nations. The kind of culture that lay at the base of British national identity was one of achievement, of technical superiority which led Britain to dominate the seas and to be the leading industrial and military power, and enable her through her empire to take her civilisation to the rest of the world. Great Britain relied less upon a racial or linguistic sense of the nation than some other countries, but the English language was nevertheless prominent as a unifying force, and racist thinking was by no means unfamiliar to the British. The whole concept of empire was closely linked to a notion of British superiority and the 'white man's burden' of carrying civilisation to the savages of the rest of the world.

What differed between British national feeling after the end of the Napoleonic wars and that of the other European nations we have examined so far was the relatively unimportant role of opposition to other specific nations in the definition of self. The Hungarians and Czechs, for example, were at least in part defined as not Austrian. The British, however, defined themselves geographically as separate from the continent, and were less prone to think of themselves in terms of criteria that distinguished them from each of their neighbours. Their culture, language, history and race were present, but the British did not develop them into a national mythology to the extent that we have seen over the last few chapters in the rest of Europe. Instead the British relied much more heavily on geography (insularity) and overall economic strength and success. This did not mean that the British did not invent traditions and create a national myth after 1870 like other nations; only that in doing so they were able to focus more intensely on the greatness of the empire which had already been achieved.

For Britain, as for other European nations, 1870 represented a point of transition between the attitudes towards the nation and also towards the empire. In the early part of the nineteenth century, the British Empire remained relatively stable in size, and the emphasis on liberalism meant that the politics of expansion of empire were relatively out of fashion and industrial development was the primary focus. By 1870, as economic and political conditions changed with the coming of a global economic recession, and free trade and liberalism correspondingly decreased in popularity, imperialism took off with renewed vigour. Promoted by such leaders as Benjamin Disraeli, the British Empire gained a previously unprecedented popularity. Previously hostile to the idea of empire, Disraeli changed his mind and became one of its most staunch supporters. In a famous policy speech at the Crystal Palace in 1872, he denounced the Liberals for opposing and weakening the empire and set the tone for the next few decades of British foreign and imperial policy (see Document 7.1). A new period of imperial expansion began, which it was hoped would guarantee British economic prospects for the foreseeable future. The expansion was also in part a response to the rivalry of the other European nations who were embarking on imperial projects, made in order to maintain the primary position of Britain and ensure that the most strategic points and the most valuable colonies were reserved for it alone.

As 1870–1914 was the age of popular nationalism, in Britain it was also the age of popular imperialism. With the renewed government interest in the empire came a policy of promotion of the imperial ideal on a national scale, leading to greater popularity for the empire and imperial expansion. Children learned about the empire in schools, and the empire became an object of attention and pride for all classes of society. At such events as Queen Victoria's jubilees, the empire figured prominently in the symbols and ceremonies designed to promote and popularise the British nation. Britishness and the idea of British civilisation were highly valued, and the missionary zeal promoted through imperialism was extremely patriotic in character. Thus the national image or identity developed in Britain was an imperial one, and the fulfilment of the British nation was to export the ideals of Britishness to the colonies.

British national character was linked to the sense of Britishness and of empire and was, as we saw briefly in the preceding chapter, untainted by national humiliation. While other nations turned to national self-affirmation, and to imperial expansion as a way of compensating for real or perceived defeats and weaknesses leading to a sense of national failure, Britain remained the most powerful and successful nation throughout the nineteenth century. It was the very success of the British that coloured the national image; Britain ruled the waves, British civilisation was clearly superior, as demonstrated by the industrial and military successes throughout the period.

France

In France, nationalism was more significant as a cause or motivation for imperialism than it was for Britain. After their defeat of 1870–71 in the Franco-Prussian war, the French turned to the building of a colonial empire in an attempt to bring confidence back to the nation and to preserve France's position as a 'great power'. One of the major figures in the creation and development of the French colonial empire was Jules Ferry, a republican politician who was most famous for the introduction of free, compulsory and lay schools throughout France. It was also he who framed the republican policy of imperialism. In a speech which he delivered in 1885, he explained to the other republicans in the Chamber of Deputies that a colonial empire was imperative if France was to retain its status as a first-rank world power (see Document 7.2). A key element of the text is the preoccupation with France's status among nations and France's rivalry with other European nations as the motivating factors behind the policy of expansion. National greatness was central to the republican concept of French national identity, and the development of a colonial empire was merely an important means to maintain their sense of grandeur and importance in world affairs.

Even in the French concept of the civilising mission, French national identity appears as a motivating factor for imperial expansion. The 'civilisation' that France hoped to export to the rest of the world and to bring to the native populations of its colonies was a republican ideal, based on the rights of man as they had been conceived during the French Revolution. It was also closely linked to the French language and culture, which to its people epitomised civilisation. It was France's own national image and culture that the French hoped to take to the colonies, and if their duty was to enlighten the uncivilised, the means was national. The greatness of France and the desirability of its national culture were considered as unquestionable, and it was an intrinsic part of the French concept of France that its people were the pioneers of the doctrine of the rights of man. It was therefore up to them to see that this doctrine was brought to all oppressed peoples in the world, as a witness both to its rightness and to French national glory.

Not only were nationalism and the nature of French identity factors contributing to the pursuit of colonies and the development of imperialism, but France also differed from Britain in the subsequent influence of imperialism on the nation and the national identity. The notion of France as an imperial power, and the role of the colonies in shaping the French national image, were considerably less important than similar factors were in Great Britain. France defined itself in terms of its language and its history, with special reference to the revolution, and its colonies were never more than peripheral as a defining characteristic. Throughout the period of imperial expansion, France always had a strong internal contingent opposed to the acquisition of an empire, who asserted that France did not need colonies and that she had everything necessary for greatness within her European borders. By 1940, the longevity of the French Empire meant that it had become at least a small part of the national self-image, and that the French thought of themselves as having colonies and engaging in imperialism, but the empire never came close to the centrality and primacy it held for Great Britain.

Germany

Throughout most of the nineteenth century, the rulers in Germany were more preoccupied with internal politics or unification than with building a colonial empire, and after unification in 1871 Bismarck's policy remained oriented towards continental Europe. He encouraged the French to seek colonies in order to prevent thoughts of revenge, diverting their attention away from the territory of Alsace and Lorraine which had recently been taken over by Germany. At the same time, however, he was not interested in acquiring colonies for Germany. Thinking that the colonies were not really of any economic benefit, Bismarck preferred to concentrate his efforts in foreign policy on seeking European alliances and making sure that France remained isolated and in no position to threaten what he hoped would be Germany's predominant position in the continent of Europe. Thus at the beginning of the 1870s German nationalism was focused internally, and seemed unlikely to develop imperialist tendencies.

By the mid-1880s, however, Bismarck's policy towards imperial expansion changed, and Germany entered the group of European powers seeking colonies in the rest of the world. This change of attitude did not come about because Bismarck had become convinced that colonies were necessary to Germany economically, but primarily because of the way internal politics were developing in the newly united German Reich. By associating colonial expansion with glory for the German nation and true patriotism, Bismarck was able to use imperialism as a platform to accuse his opponents of, if not treason, at least an insufficient patriotic spirit. This change of policy was essentially a means to retain power; Bismarck never became an enthusiastic imperialist. Imperial expansion remained as one element in a foreign policy oriented chiefly towards Europe, designed to retain the support of those who thought that Germany needed a colonial empire either for economic reasons or to enhance national glory and standing. Hence German pursuit of colonies began for reasons similar to those of France, in order to demonstrate and further promote the glory of the nation, and as a means of attracting the attention and support of the population. The German example indicates that in the Europe of the late nineteenth century, a strong sense of nationalism tended to lead to imperialism since even in situations where imperialism was not considered particularly beneficial economically, it was still held to be necessary. Imperialism was a consequence of the struggle for power and greatness among the major European nations.

With Bismarck's fall from power in 1890, Germany's pursuit of colonies continued with even greater enthusiasm. In 1896 William II unveiled the *Weltpolitik* or 'world policy', his plan for a pre-eminent role for Germany in world affairs. It included the acquisition of colonies. Germany participated in the scramble for Africa, and also secured several island colonies in the south Pacific. In spite of this activity, imperial development had little impact upon the German national image. It is not as significant in national memories, mythology and literature as in France and much less significant than in Great Britain. This is partly due to the fact that Germany acquired colonies later than these other countries. Since they were taken away after the First World War, Germany was a colonial power for a relatively short time, and was inevitably less influenced by the experience.

Germany was also an 'empire' within its European boundaries, and therefore the word itself had national connotations. For this reason, a German speaking of the empire probably meant simply Germany, rather than Germany and its colonies. Finally, the German definition of the nation was centred more closely upon race than it was in either of the two other cases discussed so far, and the possible contributions of a colonial empire to the nation were therefore more limited. In summary, the relationship between nationalism and imperialism in Germany was similar to that in France; the possession of colonies was a good way to increase the prestige of the nation and demonstrate the nation's importance in the world. Imperialism made an even smaller impact, however, upon the national identity than it did in France.

Other countries

Several other European countries had colonies outside Europe during these years. Italy sought to gain colonies for much the same reasons as France and Germany: to increase national glory and to prove that it was among the first rank of nations. Defeat at the hands of Ethiopia confirmed Italy's inability to achieve the same level of success as either of the others, and their colonial expansion remained on a smaller scale. Spurred on by Leopold II, Belgium colonised the Congo, but acquisition of the colony remained more a matter of personal prestige for the king than of greater glory for the Belgian nation. The Netherlands held the islands of Indonesia, possessions which they retained from an earlier phase of colonial expansion, but these had a limited impact upon the development of Dutch national identity. In Spain, this period was one of colonial loss and reduction of total territory, although it sought to acquire some new land in Morocco. For all of these nations, the push towards imperialism was partly a matter of seeking glory for their nation, or was at least motivated by an impulse to imitate the actions of the greater nations and compete with them on a lesser level and a smaller scale.

In conclusion, what can be said of the links between nationalism and imperialism? It is clear that nationalism, in the sense of national pride and the quest for glory for the nation, did contribute to the drive for imperial expansion. The competition and rivalry which grew between the different nations of Europe in the latter part of the nineteenth century led some to seek colonies as a means of demonstrating the greatness of their own nation. The belief that existing national characteristics embodied an ideal of civilisation which it was their duty to export and promote as a form of enlightenment for the rest of the world enhanced the other reasons behind the civilising mission. Writing in 1902, J. A. Hobson considered that imperialism was a perversion of nationalism, which in its 'natural' form was a desire for independence and a promotion of distinctive cultures (see Document 7.3). Through the unnecessary, aggressive competition between nations within Europe or over colonies outside it, the two concepts were linked in a way that threatened peace and stability. It would be an exaggeration to claim that nationalism was the sole or even the principal motivating factor behind imperial expansion, but nationalism undeniably added to the other arguments in favour of it, and in that way it made its own small contribution to the European phenomenon of imperialism.

Imperialism's impact upon the nations, national identities and nationalist ideology varied according to the country in question. The impact was strongest in the greatest of the imperial nations, Great Britain, where the role of the empire in national imagery was a prominent one. For the other European nations – while the colonies may have been thought important economically or militarily, or for reasons of national prestige – their contribution to national identities was more marginal, and in many cases of short duration.

The imperialist nation

7.1 Excerpt from a speech by Benjamin Disraeli at the Crystal Palace, 24 June 1872

Gentlemen, there is another and second great object of the Tory party. If the first is to maintain the institutions of the country, the second is, in my opinion, to uphold the empire of England. If you look at the history of this country since the advent of Liberalism – forty years ago – you will find that there has been no effort, so continuous, so subtle, supported by so much energy, and carried on with so much ability and acumen, as the attempts of Liberalism to effect the disintegration of the empire of England.

. . .

[T]hose who advised this policy – and I believe their convictions were sincere – looked upon the Colonies of England, looked even upon our connection with India, as a burden upon this country, viewing everything in a financial aspect, and totally passing by those moral and political considerations which make nations great, and by the influence of which alone men are distinguished from animals . . . [W]ith respect to . . . the maintenance of the empire – public opinion appears to be in favour of our principles – public opinion which, I am bound to say, thirty years ago, was not favourable to our principles.

. . .

I tell all who are here present that there is a responsibility which you have incurred today, and which you must meet like men. When you return to your homes, when you return to your counties and your cities, you must tell to all those whom you can influence that the time is at hand, that, at least, it cannot be far distant, when England will have to decide between national and cosmopolitan principles. The issue is not a mean one. It is whether you will be content to be a comfortable England, modelled and moulded upon the Continental principles and meeting in due course an inevitable fate, or whether you will be a great country – an Imperial country – a country where your sons, when they rise, rise to paramount positions, and obtain not merely the esteem of their countrymen, but command the respect of the world.

Source: T. E. Kebbel (ed.), *Selected speeches of the late Right Honourable the Earl of Beaconsfield*, vol. II, London, 1882, pp. 523–35

7.2 Excerpt from a speech by Jules Ferry in the French Chamber of Deputies, 28 July 1885

The real question, gentlemen, the question which needs to be asked, and asked in the clearest of terms, is the following: must the reflection engaged in by nations which have suffered greatly result in abdication? And because a detestable policy, visionary and blind, has thrown France into the situation you know well, must the governments which inherited this unfortunate situation condemn themselves to never again engage in European politics? Preoccupied with the contemplation of this wound which will bleed for ever, will they let everything go, will they let anyone besides ourselves establish themselves in Tunis, or police the mouth of the Red River? . . . Will they allow others to fight over the regions of equatorial Africa? Will they allow others to settle Egyptian affairs, which in so many ways are really French? I know, gentlemen, that this theory exists, I know that it is expressed by sincere minds, which believe that henceforth France should have policies restricted to Europe alone . . .

Gentlemen, in Europe as it stands, in this competition with so many rivals expanding around us, some through military or naval improvements, others through the prodigious development of an ever-growing population; in such a Europe, or even in such a universe, a policy of reflection or abstention is simply the road to decadence! The nations of our time cannot be great except through the activity which they develop themselves . . .

To be influential without acting, without involvement in world affairs, remaining on the sidelines of European designs, considering all expansion in Africa and the Orient as a trap or a simple adventure; for a great nation to live like that is, believe it well, to abdicate responsibility, and in a shorter time than you can imagine, to fall from the first rank to the third or fourth.

Source: G. Pervillé, *De l'Empire français à la décolonisation*, Paris, 1991; trans. T. Baycroft

7.3 Excerpt from *Imperialism: a study* by J. A. Hobson

During the nineteenth century the struggle towards nationalism, or the establishment of political union on a basis of nationality, was a dominant factor alike in dynastic movements and as an inner motive in the life of masses of population . . . This was the most definite achievement of the nineteenth century . . . The close of the third quarter of the century saw Europe fairly settled into large national States or federations of States . . .

This passion and the dynamic forms it helped to mould and animate are largely attributable to the fierce prolonged resistance which peoples, both great and small, were called on to maintain against the imperial designs of Napoleon . . .

It is a debasement of this genuine nationalism, by attempts to overflow its natural banks and absorb the near or distant territory of reluctant and unassimilable peoples, that marks the passage from nationalism to a spurious colonialism on the one hand, Imperialism on the other . . .

The novelty of recent Imperialism regarded as a policy consists chiefly in its adoption by several nations. The notion of a number of competing empires is essentially modern . . .

Nationalism is a plain highway to internationalism, and if it manifests divergence we may well suspect a perversion of its nature and purpose. Such a perversion is Imperialism, in which nations trespassing beyond the limits of facile assimilation transform the wholesome stimulative rivalry of varied national types into the cut-throat struggle of competing empires . . .

A nationalism that bristles with resentment and is all astrain with the passion of self-defence is only less perverted from its natural genius than the nationalism which glows with the animus of greed and self-aggrandisement at the expense of others. From this aspect aggressive Imperialism is an artificial stimulation of nationalism in peoples too foreign to be absorbed and too compact to be permanently crushed . . . The older nationalism was primarily an inclusive sentiment; its natural relation to the same sentiment in other people was lack of sympathy, not open hostility; there was no inherent antagonism to prevent nationalities from growing and thriving side by side. Such in the main was the nationalism of the earlier nineteenth century, and the politicians of Free Trade had some foundation for their dream of a quick growth of effective, informal internationalism by peaceful, profitable intercommunication of goods and ideas among nations recognising a just harmony of interests in free peoples.

The overflow of nationalism into imperial channels quenched all such hopes . . .

Though the conduct of nations in dealing with one another has commonly been determined at all times by selfish and short-sighted considerations, the conscious, deliberate adoption of this standard at an age when the intercourse of nations and their interdependence for all essentials of human life grow ever closer, is a retrograde step fraught with grave perils to the cause of civilisation . . .

The political effects, actual and necessary, of the new Imperialism, as illustrated in the case of the greatest of imperialist Powers, may be thus summarised. It is a constant menace to peace, by furnishing continual temptations to further aggression upon lands occupied by lower races and by embroiling our nation with other nations of rival imperial ambitions; to the sharp peril of war it adds the chronic danger and degradation of militarism, which not merely wastes the current physical and moral resources of the nations, but checks the very course of civilisation . . . Finally, the spirit, the policy, and the methods of Imperialism are hostile to the institutions of popular self-government, favouring forms of political tyranny and social authority which are the deadly enemies of effective liberty and equality.

Source: J. A. Hobson, *Imperialism: a study*, London, 1902

Document case-study questions

1 Account for similarities and differences in the tone and content of Documents 7.1 and 7.2.

2 What is the key motivating factor behind imperial expansion in Documents 7.1 and 7.2, and what is the relationship to nationalism?

3 In what ways is imperialism a perversion of nationalism according to Document 7.3?

4 In what ways does the vision of internationalism in Document 7.3 differ from that of Document 5.1? How do you account for the fact that the final sentence of Document 7.3 declares that imperialism is opposed to liberty and equality, which were fundamental principles in the idea of the nation as it was originally developed?

8 Nationalism in conflict, 1914–1945

The twentieth century saw nationalism bring conflict to Europe and to the world. Major conflicts occurred between nations, within nations, and over the ideological nature of nationalism and the theories behind it. There were military wars, political battles and social struggles as well as intellectual and ideological contention, and a fight between opposing leaders for the loyalty of the populations. The phase of popular nationalism had seen competition and aggression between nations, but during the period from 1914 to 1945, with two massive world wars at either end, the European nations witnessed violence and hardship as never before. This chapter will examine the various conflicts in order to understand the contribution of nationalism to them as well as how they in turn affected nationalist thinking.

The First World War

The outbreak of the First World War in 1914 brought a huge initial patriotic outburst on the part of the populations of the belligerent states. Volunteers rallied to the armed forces at the first announcement of war, and men and women on both sides were proud, confident and cheerful at the thought of a quick victory, anticipating honour and glory for their nation. The call to arms was accompanied by a great deal of patriotic national propaganda, such as the famous Kitchener recruitment poster, 'Your country needs you!' (see illustration on p. 72). The policies described earlier of teaching national culture and encouraging the development of a strong sense of national identity and loyalty among the masses (see Chapters 3 and 4) had undoubtedly succeeded. All over Europe, the nation-states could, by 1914, rely on a strong base of popular patriotic support. It has even been claimed that this show of patriotism demonstrated the victory of the nation over class in terms of winning the loyalty and the hearts of the people, and represented one of the highest points of nationalism. The socialists and communists had hoped that international working-class solidarity would prevent war and lead instead to revolution, but when the crunch came men obeyed the call to arms and fought for their nations against their working-class 'brothers'.

The victory of the nation was not as complete as the initial reaction to the declaration of war would suggest, however. The war was not over quickly, and as the months dragged on into years, and the full horror of the reality of trench warfare set in, the wisdom of the war was called into question and the early

Kitchener recruitment poster, Britain, First World War. This poster encouraged men to enlist in the British army, stressing the sense of individual duty to the nation. How does this poster draw upon nationalist feeling?

"YOUR COUNTRY NEEDS YOU"

unwavering loyalty to the nation was tempered by frustration and dissent. Several of the belligerent nations experienced social unrest, there were mutinies of soldiers in 1917, and the tsar of Russia was overthrown by a communist revolution. The people were only willing to put up with a certain amount of hardship and suffering in the name of the nation before they would protest, quietly at first and then more loudly. Not many went so far as to question the validity of the nation itself while the hostilities were still going on, but the lengths to which they would go, and the sacrifices they were prepared to make in the name of patriotism and for the glory of the nation, had a limit.

Versailles and the national map of Europe

At the conclusion of the First World War, the principles which were used as the basis of the peace settlement demonstrated how powerful the idea of the nation had become. The Fourteen Points of President Woodrow Wilson of the United States included several specific recommendations for the settlement of disputes which pointed the way to the autonomy of nations (see Document 8.1). He was concerned that, at the end of the war, the peace settlement should include provision for the re-establishment of Poland as a separate nation-state, for the former Austro-Hungarian and Ottoman Empires to be divided into states along the lines of nationality, and for the smaller nation-states which had been occupied during the course of the war to be evacuated and re-established. The principle of the self-determination of peoples, of nations, lay at the heart of these concerns. Wilson's Fourteen Points were used as the basis for the peace treaty which was signed at the end of the war in Versailles in 1919, and an attempt was made to use nationality as the basis for the readjustment of borders. This overwhelming acceptance on all sides that 'nationality' should determine which areas had the right to form a separate state, and the principle that 'the people' should have some say in their own political fate, marked the full-scale victory of the idea of the nation in Europe.

While the decision to redraw much of the map of Europe on the basis of nationality seemed a good idea, in practice this proved far from straightforward, and it was impossible to achieve completely. The different races, religions and language groups in central and eastern Europe were not neatly distributed, each in their own territory, but were intermingled in most areas. Wilson's point that the frontiers of Italy should be readjusted along the 'clearly recognisable lines of nationality' was impossible to realise. When one slice of territory was transferred from the Austro-Hungarian Empire to Italy, what was previously an Italian-speaking minority joined the majority, but at the same time the transfer left a Slavic minority in Italy.

Not only was division according to nationality overly intricate and unmanageable in practice, but other principles occasionally entered the discussions and took precedence. Access to the sea was considered to be indispensable for several of the previously landlocked nations, such as Poland and Serbia. This meant taking a slice out of Germany and giving it to Poland, thus dividing the German nation in two; and creating Yugoslavia, which combined several 'nationalities' in one state. Thus the theory of 'one nation – one state' was difficult to put into practice. Occasionally it had to give way to other political concerns, but it was nevertheless accepted almost universally as a basic principle by the end of the First World War.

In addition to the new European nations emerging from the treaty of Versailles, the Irish Free State also secured its independence in the aftermath of the war. Following a long struggle throughout the nineteenth century for national independence from Great Britain, and a deferred promise from the war years, the Government of Ireland Act was finally passed by the British parliament in 1920. It called for the separation of Ireland in two, with one parliament for the northern counties, referred to as Ulster, and another for the south, to be called the Irish Free State. Both parts were to remain under the British crown. This received some support in the Free State, but groups opposed to partition and to the necessity of swearing loyalty to the British monarch embarked on an armed rebellion of short duration. Periodic violence and sustained opposition between the two sides continued into the 1930s, when the Free State and Britain embarked on a fierce tariff war. Ireland gradually won greater autonomy, and eventually became a fully independent republic, electing its first president in 1938.

National organisation

As the nation became more accepted as an organising principle, the 20-year period that followed the First World War also saw the nation-states take on more practical significance in the organisation of social and economic life. While it was true that there were 'national' economies during the nineteenth century, there was also a large following for the liberal doctrine of free trade and minimal government regulation of the economy was considered desirable. The 1920s and 1930s were characterised by a shift in the policy of the nation-states; they became more interventionist and isolationist, or in a sense more national. The increased social tension beginning in the latter stages of the nineteenth century – which reached new heights during the war – combined with the fear of communist revolutions as had been seen in Russia, encouraged the nation-states to develop their social policies, and do something definite about social problems. This meant greater regulation of working conditions and hours, and in several (but not all) cases the extension of the franchise to women.

The national economies became subject to much greater regulation as well. The war had taught governments that some degree of centralised economic planning was necessary – not as much as during the war itself, but more than had been felt to be desirable during the nineteenth century. More tightly controlled monetary policy, the increased presence of tariffs, the regulation of migration through the introduction of work permits, and the general regulation of the economy through government intervention, monitoring and economic planning all became more commonplace. In short, economies became much more 'national' than they had been in the past, with the governments of the nation-states intervening to ensure that each nation could be relatively independent economically, encouraging the development of diverse industries which could look after all of the nation's needs. Even Great Britain, the most prominent supporter of free trade and liberalism throughout the nineteenth century, experienced this transition and found it necessary to tolerate some level of intervention on the part of the national state authorities in the economic affairs of the country. In one sense it would seem that during the inter-war period the different nations chose to retreat into isolation rather than risk open competition which would put them at risk.

If, at the end of the First World War, the nation as an organising principle was more widely accepted than ever before, and the nation-states themselves became more independent and integrated socially and economically, that did not mean that no awareness remained of the dangers of too much unrestrained, ambitious nationalism. On the contrary, the lesson of the horrors of mass wars in the twentieth century was crystal clear. The danger of too much competitive nationalism, which could lead to such a war, was equally apparent to everyone.

The League of Nations

Because of the fear of war, an attempt was made to reduce the competitive element between nations through the creation of an international association with the goal of maintaining peaceful relations and facilitating co-operation. It was called the League of Nations. Based on the fourteenth of President Wilson's points, the league was to act as a guarantee of collective security, so that all the nations would agree that any act of aggression by one particular nation against another would be resisted collectively by all of the others (see Document 8.1). The threat of opposition and resistance by *all* of the other world nations, it was hoped, would be enough to discourage anyone from starting another large-scale war, or even from attempting to annex a small territory from one of the smaller or weaker states. In this way the security of all nations from aggression – even the small, recently created ones which were necessarily weaker and more vulnerable – would be guaranteed by the co-operation of the members of the league.

The story of why the League of Nations failed in its objectives to safeguard the world from the aggression of competing nations and to prevent national rivalry from leading to hostility and war is well known. From the beginning the United States refused to join, in spite of the fact that it was the US president who had conceived the initial idea and who had pushed hard to get it accepted at the peace conference. When Wilson returned after the signing of the treaty of Versailles, the American Senate refused to ratify the treaty and there was nothing Wilson could do to persuade them otherwise. Without the participation of the United States, the greatly weakened League of Nations was not taken seriously enough, by its members as well as those outside, to have a real impact on international relations. It became apparent that none of the nations was really ready to commit itself to collective security, certainly not to the point of individual sacrifice that was required for the system to be effective as a deterrent to aggression.

In addition to, and in parallel with, the League of Nations, several attempts were made during the inter-war period to oppose the aggressiveness of competing nations and to reduce the risk of future conflicts. Since one of the main threats to the peace settlement was the tension and opposition between the two large nations of France and Germany, it was thought that one possible way to alleviate future nationalist tension would be to bring those two nations in particular closer together. During the 1920s the respective foreign ministers of the two countries – Aristide Briand, a former prime minister, for France and Gustav Stresemann for Germany – sought to remedy the situation themselves through as much reconciliation and co-operation as was possible. In 1925 they negotiated the Locarno pact, a treaty of mutual non-aggression which also permitted Germany to join the League of Nations in 1926 and paved the way to further agreements on both the strategic and the economic fronts. Both participated in the negotiations which led to the Kellogg–Briand pact in 1928, in which 57 countries condemned war as an instrument of policy. For a short time in the final years of the 1920s it appeared that the policy of reconciliation might actually develop into a relatively lasting peace, and some of those who followed Stresemann and Briand were hopeful. Their deaths, in 1929 and 1932 respectively, together with the influences of the economic depression in the 1930s, lingering dislike, mutual distrust, resentment, national feelings of rivalry on both sides and finally the coming to power of the Nazis in 1933, made the prevention of nationalist tensions from eventually resurfacing impossible.

Pacifism

Some Europeans during the inter-war period went so far as to oppose the idea of patriotism to the nation, which led inevitably to conflict and war, and developed a doctrine of pacifism. Some were those who put faith in the collective security of the League of Nations and hoped that in addition to international co-operation, the way of the future would be through anti-militarism. While pacifists were not internationalist or anti-national in the same explicit way that the socialists and communists were (see Chapter 5), their theory was nevertheless seen to contradict patriotic nationalism through its all-out opposition to military violence. If we examine the extract from *The necessity of pacifism* by John Middleton Murry, we see that he does not claim that patriotism is wrong, only that it is futile (see Document 8.2). He claimed that war had lost its purpose, and that military spending got in the way of social spending, paralysing the true development of the nation.

The pacifist point of view was criticised emphatically by nationalists calling themselves patriots, who still believed in the necessity of defence for the nation, militarily or otherwise, and maintained that war still had this vital purpose in international relations. By the inter-war period, even mainstream national patriotism had grown to resemble aspects of the right-wing variety of nationalism which appeared in the popular phase at the end of the nineteenth century, for which the rivalry between nations and the glory of one nation in opposition to others remained significant. The pacifists' refusal to join the armed forces, their criticism of patriotism and the belief that any war was evil and not necessary aroused the anger of militant nationalists, who accused them of betrayal, disloyalty or even treason.

The class-based theory, which had already been opposed to the idea of the nation for some time, continued to be used to criticise nations and national organisation during the inter-war period. International communism maintained the doctrine that nations should not be followed and believed that loyalty should be owed instead to one's class. Following the victory of the Russian Revolution and the very serious social tension in Germany in the post-war years, the communists had higher hopes that an international proletarian revolution would succeed. Indeed, in 1918 the menace of a communist revolution, not only in Germany but also in various other western European countries, was one that had to be taken seriously. Even when the possibility of the outbreak of a proletarian revolution was reduced with the passing of time, popular support for communism within the western European nations nevertheless remained a significant presence during the inter-war period.

Fascism

As happened in response to the pacifist critique of the nation, this rise in the popularity of communism had a tendency to encourage the extreme nationalists to shout even more loudly that the nation was being undermined by the disloyalty of communists taking their orders from Moscow. In several instances the rise of the left contributed to the rise of an even more nationalist, war-mongering extreme right. This is the same right as described above, which followed the tradition of nationalism going back to the late nineteenth century, focusing upon the exclusivity and uniqueness of the nation as opposed to all others. This nationalism was more conflictual and tended towards authoritarianism, giving rise to the inter-war fascist movements. Several nations saw the fascists take over control of the state, using nationalist rhetoric and providing nationalist solutions to the problems created by the social and economic tensions which characterised the inter-war period.

The first of the nations to succumb to the fascist nationalists was Italy. Led by Benito Mussolini, the Italian fascists gained power in 1922. Examination of the text of Mussolini's Naples speech delivered on 14 October 1922 (see Document 8.3) reveals striking use of nationalist rhetoric. He acknowledged that the nation and the greatness of the nation were both myths, and yet he called for the subordination of everything else to the achievement of this greatness. He used the belief that following him, through strong authoritarian leadership, Italy could translate national greatness 'into a total reality'. Force was an important part of his plan, and in order to achieve greatness he wanted to encourage his followers to turn the force of the spirit into real force. The themes which he associated with the nation – force, grandeur, greatness of the spirit – are all values which necessitate and lead inevitably to conflict, both theoretical and real, with other nations. Mussolini identified himself and the Italian nation with the greater glory of imperial Rome, in both his words and the images surrounding him.

In Spain, a nationalist uprising led by General Franco began in 1936 and emerged victorious from the Spanish Civil War. A republic since 1930, Spain had been subjected to a great deal of internal tension between a republican left and a clerical right. Coups had been attempted by both the right and the communists before Franco's nationalist rebellion began. His nationalism was of a fascist, authoritarian variety, and he was supported by fascist Italy and Germany in the civil war. Only the Soviet Union openly opposed Franco; France, Britain and the other great powers preferred to declare themselves officially neutral. In the tense climate of the 1930s, it was the strong, aggressive nationalist stance that won the day.

Germany had struggled through extreme social and economic hardship during the 1920s, experiencing a complete monetary collapse along the way to a limited recovery by the end of the decade, all the while remaining a democracy. It was not until the depression came and economic troubles continued that they turned, in 1933, to Adolf Hitler and the national socialists. Like Mussolini's Italian fascists, the Nazis came to power with a programme of rebuilding national greatness, of reclaiming Germany's rightful place in world affairs, and of avenging the defeat of 1918 through remilitarisation and advanced economic and technological development and modernisation. In a speech given at the end of 1933, one of Hitler's leading lieutenants, Joseph Goebbels, explained the nationalist stance of their party (see Document 8.4). He claimed that his party's rise to power represented a revolution 'from below' which had as its goal that of making the German nation 'into a single people'. Knowing that this foreshadows the great drive for racial purification attempted during the Second World War, we can nevertheless see here how this future policy had its origins in the racial concept of the German nation which had been gradually developed over the whole course of the nineteenth century, dating at the very least as far back as Fichte in 1807 (see Chapter 2). German nationalism had by the 1930s reached a point at which rivalry and conflict, as well as the rejection of the non-German 'other', had become the fundamental aspect of the German idea of the nation.

In addition to the racial definition of the nation, Goebbels stressed the role of art as a key element in national greatness. Mussolini had also alluded to art and philosophy as a more critical measure of the immortality of states than their territorial size. In both cases it is the cultural dimension of national identity which has become the area of conflict. The goal was to demonstrate that their nation's cultural achievements were greater than others, more deserving of praise and merit, and at least on a par with the great civilisations of the past. What began as a concept of the nation and a way to define the nation was used to increase the competition and rivalry between nations.

The inter-war period can be seen as a time in which the idea of the nation was more widely accepted than it had ever been in history. It was the official doctrine of the majority of states, was widely popular among their populations and had been used as the basis of the peace settlement for redrawing the map of Europe after the First World War. Since it was accepted by all but a few pacifist or communist objectors, who remained in the minority, conflict within nations no longer took the form of pushing the idea of the nation into the forefront, but of convincing electors that one's party was the most 'national'. The attempt in the aftermath of the war and throughout the 1920s to moderate excessive nationalism within the nation-states through reform, and to limit its potential dangers through the development of international organisations and treaties, was to fail. The right-wing nationalists, who had been around since the end of the nineteenth century, were able to take a leading position in several European nations through the kind of rhetoric we find in the speeches of Mussolini and Goebbels. Their influence was strong enough to enable them to use the patriotic and national myths which were already popular in order to support their policies of violence, aggression and expansion. These policies ultimately brought most of Europe and the world back into a war of nations between 1939 and 1945.

After the acceptance by the international community of Hitler's invasion of Austria and of the Sudetenland in Czechoslovakia, both in the name of pan-Germanic ideals, it was finally realised that German national ambition would not come to an end easily when the German army invaded Poland on 1 September 1939. It can be said that the allies' aim in finally standing up for Poland in 1939 was to defend the basic principle of the integrity of the nations within Europe that had been established after 1918. But not only was this stance adopted too late, it was also at first a resounding military failure that led to an early German triumph.

The Second World War

The Second World War was fought in conditions very different from those of the First. Military technology had developed, and the stalemate trench warfare of 1914–18 was replaced by a war of movement, of quick striking tanks and of aeroplanes. The German war machine wiped out most of central Europe and France within the first year's fighting. With Great Britain remaining as the principal opponent to Germany, it looked very much as if it would be Hitler's Europe, in which there would be a clearly defined racial-national hierarchy, that would come out of the war victorious. In the name of desiring racial purity for the German nation, before the war was over the Nazis had already embarked on the Holocaust, a campaign of extermination of all Jews and gypsies within the territory they held.

After the German attack on its former ally the Soviet Union, and the entry of the United States into the war, the Germans and their Italian allies fought the remainder of the war on several fronts. The fighting continued for several years and the allied forces were victorious in the end. While the rhetoric of the war on the allied side was in some ways less 'national' than it had been in the First World War – instead of fighting for the honour and glory of their country they were fighting to defend freedom – the question of national prestige was never completely put aside. This was particularly true for the smaller allies, such as General Charles de Gaulle's Free France and the Polish government exiled in London, who undoubtedly fought for the honour and even the survival of their own nations.

National glory was certainly one of the principal motivating factors for war on the part of the axis powers, and it did also influence some of the larger of the allies. In the Soviet Union, posters displayed at the time reveal nationalist feeling within the war propaganda. In the first of the two shown (see illustration on p. 80), a soldier asks, 'What have you done for the Front?' It is reminiscent of the British First World War recruitment poster, hinting that soldiers are needed. The factory smoke stacks and workers in the background indicate that those behind the lines should work hard to support those who are actually fighting. In the second poster, a historical parallel is drawn between the Soviet and the Russian nations, suggesting both continuity and greatness. In the foreground is the contemporary situation, which recalls 1812 through a shadow. Hitler is being knocked down by the larger-than-life Soviet gun, just as Napoleon was pushed back by the Russian pitchforks. The message is clear: there is a national threat; and an optimistic rallying call is made through a reminder of a great past victory. The poster shows that even Hitler can be defeated, just as Napoleon was before him, once the people stand firm.

Two Soviet posters.

'You – What have you done for the Front?' A Soviet poster calling for all workers to support the war effort. Compare and contrast the Soviet and British posters in terms of their messages and their use of national symbolism.

The driving of Hitler back, just as Napoleon was driven back in 1812. How does this poster suggest the greatness of the Russian/Soviet nation?

In summary, the period of nationalism in conflict began and ended with massive world wars, fought in great measure for national glory. In the period separating the two wars, conflict was never absent from the European scene, both within nations and between nations. The principle of the nation as the basis for the formation of the state was widely accepted, and internal forces rivalled one another in their claims to be the most loyal, the most patriotic or, in short, the most national. Through both war and peace, the whole period from 1914 to 1945 was characterised by conflict in the name of the defence and glory of the nation.

Looking back at the evolution of the idea of the nation and what it represented for those who developed it, what we saw in the period of nationalism in conflict was quite far removed from the original concept of the nation during the French Revolution and its aftermath. The racist, exclusive, emotional definitions of identity, the fierce national rivalry leading to aggression versus the nation's perceived enemies, and the strong-armed authoritarian assertion that what the nation requires most is glory and greatness, do not closely resemble the belief in the equality of citizens before the law justified through the support of the people, which originally characterised the idea of the nation at the end of the eighteenth century.

Document case study
Pacifism, belligerence and the nation

8.1 Points 5–14 of Woodrow Wilson's Fourteen Points

5. A free, open-minded and absolutely impartial adjustment of all colonial claims, based upon a strict observance of the principle that in determining all such questions of sovereignty the interests of the population concerned must have equal weight with the equitable claims of the government whose title is to be determined.

6. The evacuation of all Russian territory and . . . a settlement of all questions affecting Russia.

7. Belgium . . . must be evacuated and restored.

8. All French territory should be freed and the invaded portions restored, and the wrong done to France by Prussia in 1871 in the matter of Alsace and Lorraine . . . should be righted.

9. A readjustment of the frontiers of Italy should be effected along clearly recognisable lines of nationality.

10. The peoples of Austria-Hungary . . . should be accorded the freest opportunity of autonomous development.

11. Romania, Serbia and Montenegro should be evacuated; occupied territories restored; Serbia accorded free and secure access to the sea; . . . and international guarantees of the political and economic independence and territorial integrity of the several Balkan States should be entered into.

12. The Turkish portions of the present Ottoman Empire should be assured a secure sovereignty, but the other nationalities which are now under Turkish rule should be assured . . . an absolutely unmolested opportunity of autonomous development . . .

13. An independent Polish State should be erected which should include the territories inhabited by indisputably Polish populations, which shall be assured a free and secure access to the sea.

14. A general association of nations must be formed under specific covenants for the purposes of affording mutual guarantees of political independence and territorial integrity to great and small nations alike.

8.2 Extract from *The necessity of pacifism* by John Middleton Murry

It is the international rivalries inherent in capitalism which call a halt to the process of socialisation by gradual reform. Suddenly the national expenditure on armaments, always burdensome, becomes colossal: there is no margin left for the expansion of social services. At the same time, there is the imminent menace of war which, by reason of capitalist integration and the technical progress on which that integration depends, is more deadly than ever before. The integrated capitalist society is infinitely more vulnerable by reason of its increasingly delicate organisation; and the weapons by which it is threatened are infinitely more destructive because of the advance in inventive technique. At one and the same moment there is a paralysis of the internal development of the nation, and a paralysis of the instinctive life of the social organism
. . .

Nobody knows, and practically nobody pretends to know, what is going to happen . . . One cause of this deep-seated unease is obvious, and in a sense concrete: the apprehension of the danger of war is universal . . . War in Europe today, whether it be a war of defence or aggression, involves the destruction of the social organism which makes war and makes peace. Therefore, all meaning and purpose is gone out of war. The men of this country are refusing to join the army . . . It is because the life-instinct of the social organism is warning them that the old forms of patriotism are futile, and worse.

Just as this sense of the futility of patriotism today seldom finds expression in words, so it finds no coherent expression in the form of political movement: because it is inherently anti-political . . . Perhaps meta-political would be a better word. It points and thrusts beyond politics.

Source: J. Middleton Murry, *The necessity of pacifism*, London, 1937, pp. 34–8

8.3 Extract from Benito Mussolini's Naples speech, 24 October 1922

We have created our myth. The myth is a faith, a passion. It is not necessary for it to be a reality. It is a reality in the sense that it is a stimulus, is hope, is faith, is courage. Our myth is the nation, our myth is the greatness of the nation! And to this myth, this greatness, which we want to translate into a total reality, we subordinate everything else.

For us the nation is not just territory, but something spiritual. There are States which have had immense territories and which have left no trace in human history. It is not just a question of size, because there have been minute, microscopic States in history which have bequeathed memorable, immortal specimens of art and philosophy.

The greatness of the nation is all of these qualities, all of these conditions. A nation is great when it translates into reality the force of its spirit . . . Now, therefore, we desire the greatness of the nation, both material and spiritual.

Source: R. Griffin (ed.), *Fascism*, Oxford, 1995, p. 44

8.4 Extract from Joseph Goebbels' speech 'The new tasks of German culture', 15 November 1933

The purpose of the revolution which we have carried out is the forging of the German nation into a single people. This has been the longing of all good Germans for two thousand years. Attempts had been made through legal processes countless times; each of these attempts failed. Only the fervent explosion of the national passions of our people made it possible . . . What was not possible, and often not even wanted, from above, we have achieved from below. The German people, once the most fragmented in the world, atomised into its component parts and hence condemned to impotence as a world power, since 1918 lacking in arms, and, what is worse, the will to assert its rights among world powers, rose up in a unique demonstration of its sense of national strength . . .

No one orders the new world-view to march across the stage or screen. Where it does march across them, however, we must zealously ensure that in its artistic form as well it reflects the greatness of the historical process which we have completed in the German Revolution . . .

The new national art of Germany will only enjoy respect in the world and bear witness beyond the frontiers of our country to the intense cultural dynamism of the new Germany if it is firmly and ineradicably rooted in the mother earth of the national culture which produced it. The world must discover anew what is German and genuine.

Source: R. Griffin (ed.), *Fascism*, Oxford, 1995, pp. 134–5

Document case-study questions

1 What does Document 8.1 say about international attitudes to the nation?

2 How did the states of Europe hope to avoid the excesses of nationalism during the inter-war period?

3 In what ways did the inter-war ideology of pacifism oppose the nation?

4 What does the nation mean to the writer of Document 8.3?

5 Compare and contrast the nationalist rhetoric used in Documents 8.3 and 8.4. Why do both refer to art?

9 Conclusion

There can be little doubt that the idea of the nation and the powerful sentiments that it aroused among the people of Europe had a tremendous impact upon the course of history during the period that began with the French Revolution and extended to the end of the Second World War in 1945. The European world view during the nineteenth and twentieth centuries was heavily influenced by nationalism, the belief that the nation is the only legitimate source of power, that every nation should have a state of its own, that one's own nation has inherent value above and beyond that of other nations – putting it first in matters of policy – and finally that defence of its glory and honour are essential. The European map was organised and redrawn according to the principle of one state for every nation. Nationalism provoked numerous, massive wars for independence, expansion or national glory. In seeking popular support, nations encouraged social progress in the form of education for the masses in order to integrate them more completely into the national culture. National rivalries encouraged imperialism and the expansion of European power throughout the world, increasing the influence of the European idea of the nation globally.

Even though the nation is such a powerful idea and symbol, it nevertheless defies a simple, straightforward definition which is suitable for all examples. As we have seen, the nation is a very versatile concept that can be adapted to particular circumstances and that evolves over time. The most that can be said is that a nation is a group of people who believe or imagine that they share a number of characteristics, and who gradually develop the political will to act in the name of what they have identified as their nation. The kinds of characteristics that can be identified as national include common language and culture, religion, territory, a particular version of accepted history, and race or ethnicity. In a given nation, any or all of these will be present, and collectively they make up the national identity which serves to distinguish the nation from other nations. It has been shown throughout this book that characteristics defined as national are for the most part invented, rather than natural. Even those which seem the most inflexible and pre-existing, such as race, are really only elements of a constructed national mythology that is developed gradually and are 'true' only because the nation's members believe in them. Nations can in fact be thought of as imagined communities, possessing identities refined and developed over several generations.

The idea of the nation went through different stages as it was transformed from an ideology of a reforming elite to a principle generally accepted by rulers and people alike. The first phase began with the French Revolution at the end of the eighteenth century and lasted until the fall of Napoleon in 1815. At this time, the nation was put forward to rival the divine right of kings as a legal principle and foundation of all legitimacy, and it was also combined with encouragement of an emotional attachment to the state or nation in which one lived. It was the combination of these two themes that embodied the novelty of the idea of the nation in the modern period. After the treaty of Vienna and the complete re-establishment of the absolutist monarchies opposed to the concept of the nation, its defenders became a minority in opposition who waited and gathered strength.

Throughout this phase, which lasted until 1870, the latter of the two themes, emotional adhesion to the nation, was refined and developed. Odes to the nation and other forms of 'national' art were created by the Romantics. Support for the nation as a legal concept gradually increased; and liberal, nationalist opposition threatened the established absolutist order until – through a combination of revolt and reform, separation and unification – it was able to convert much of Europe into liberal, constitutional nation-states. With the exception of a brief interlude in 1848, it was an educated, middle-class elite that supported and propagated the idea of the nation during this second major phase.

After 1870, the nationalists who had come to power in the nation-states sought to consolidate their victory over absolutism through the popularisation of support for the nation. National images and identities were refined and spread to the masses through education and the dissemination of culture, and the emotional side of nationalism was accentuated even more. It was at this time that each national image attained a new degree of sophistication. The elements that distinguished one nation from another, that set each nation up as a rival to the others, outweighed the importance of the original, more general principle of power to the people which had in many ways united the different nations in the previous phases. The more solidly entrenched the national image and culture were in the population, the more the national leaders could be sure of the support of the people, and the more intense the competition and rivalry between the nations became.

By 1914, at the end of the popular phase and the beginning of what has been called the phase of nationalism in conflict, the idea of the nation had been more or less universally accepted, and opposition to the idea of the nation as an organising principle for states was minimal. With the idea of the nation so widely acknowledged, rival groups for power within the nations each sought to prove that they were more 'national' than the others and thereby to win support for themselves. This kind of struggle heightened the competitive element between nations, and nationalism became more than ever before an ideology of conflict. At the same time a shift to the right occurred. Nationalism grew more racist and intolerant, and the heightened competition between the nations of Europe was one of the major contributing factors to the two world wars that destroyed the populations of much of their own continent and had significant global consequences.

Conclusion

The Second World War marks the end of the period of nationalism in conflict in Europe, but not the end of the idea of the nation. The sheer scale of warfare permitted by the new technology acted as a powerful deterrent, and horror at the lengths to which racist nationalism had been taken in the Holocaust meant that the will to achieve lasting international agreements of peace and co-operation was much stronger in 1945 than it had been in 1919. The body that replaced the League of Nations, the United Nations, achieved greater participation and success than its predecessor in its efforts to reduce national tensions and avoid another nationalistic total war in Europe. During the post-war years, the kind of economic and administrative centralisation that had begun in the inter-war period increased dramatically as the role of the state became increasingly important in all areas of life in the nation. Economically, socially and culturally each nation became much more homogeneous than it had been in the past, and Europe entered a period of unprecedented prosperity. Many of the European nations, more confident in the undisputed economic and cultural unity of their own nations, embarked on a project of international co-operation in the decades that followed the war, forming an association called the European Economic Community, later the European Union.

While nationalist conflict between the established European nation-states may have calmed down during the post-1945 period, claims for national independence arose from other areas. Former European colonies had learned about national self-determination from their European rulers, and used that theory to claim status as independent nations themselves, calling for decolonisation. The struggle was often long, and frequently involved armed conflict as well as negotiation. Within Europe, some new claims to distinct identity and independence arose in the form of regionalisms. In areas such as the Basque country, Flanders and Scotland, groups calling themselves nationalists increased their demands for independence, but in most cases the demands were made in a much less violent manner than had been the case in the late nineteenth and early twentieth century.

A further reason for the decline in the level of conflict between established nations in the post-Second World War era is that the European nations that claimed a heritage from the Europe of the nineteenth and early twentieth centuries came essentially from western Europe. In the east, a new revolutionary order inspired by communist doctrine had arisen to take the place of the nation as a source of conflict. Although these nations did not openly challenge the idea of the nation and remained organised in nation-states, the conflict of ideology between the communist and capitalist blocs tended to reduce the conflict between nations in each to a secondary, seemingly less significant level. This position was reinforced by the fact that in each camp the European nations came under the wing of one of the superpowers – the United States in the west and the Soviet Union in the east. Thus after 1945 the history of nationalism in Europe is not finished – we have seen that some regionalisms appeared and the struggle for decolonisation developed – but has seemed of secondary importance in the greater ideological confrontation between east and west. Since the fall of the communist bloc in the 1990s, the idea of the nation as well as nationalism seems to have returned to the European political scene, and has become a renewed source of conflict and tension in the Balkans.

This study has not pretended to be an exhaustive account of the numerous different nations that grew up in Europe between 1789 and 1945, but has aimed to provide the reader with a general history of European nationalism, underlining the different phases it went through and the overall impact it had upon the development of European civilisation. As we have seen, nationalism is a versatile ideology which adapts to local conditions and differs according to the particular ideas of the individuals at the centre of each nationalist movement. The examples provided have aimed to be the more obvious and enlightening ones for each particular period, but represent merely a selection from among the many possibilities.

Based upon the overall analysis which has been made, and the examples we have looked at, several conclusions can be drawn about the nature of nationalism in general, and its importance in the history of Europe. Examination of the historical impact of the ideology of nationalism demonstrates the considerable power and significance of ideas in history. Nationalism began in the realm of elite intellectuals as a relatively abstract theory of legitimacy, and became one of the most powerful forces, affecting all levels of society and determining the way in which people acted and ultimately even the organisation of the European state system. As it passed from one generation to another, from one region to another and from an educated elite to the masses, the idea of the nation underwent several adaptations and modifications according to the particular circumstances, so that by 1945 it had resurfaced many times in different guises, but was always recognisable as a substantial motivating force.

An ideology of the weak

It is worth noting that in every case – from the French patriots during the revolution to the German fascists in the inter-war period – nationalism was picked up and developed by social groups that were in a relatively weak position. We have already examined the contribution of humiliation to a heightened sense of nationalism and a desire to increase national prestige in the context of imperial expansion (see Chapter 7) and in the rivalry between nations, always more acute in the weaker nations that felt threatened. The same effect applies to all nationalist leaders, even those within the nation-states. This does not mean that it was the weakest groups within society that subscribed to nationalism; instead it was those individuals or groups who already possessed some limited influence or power and felt thwarted from their desire to have more.

During the French Revolution the Third Estate, relatively better educated and wealthier than they had been in the past, felt powerless within the system of the *ancien régime*, and embarked on the revolution using nationalist rhetoric in order to try to secure for themselves some power, from which they had until then been completely excluded. The real weakness of their position can be seen in the fact that they had to resort to terror in order to hold on to their position.

The first signs of nationalism in the rest of Europe sprang out of defeat at the hands of Napoleon. In the early nineteenth century, it was the lower middle class of administrators who used nationalism to encourage a shift towards their languages and away from Latin or French, the languages of the upper administration and the ruling class. They were limited in how high they could climb and in what they could achieve; they were on the fringes of high society but unable to penetrate it. Their desire to make the 'national' language a requirement can be interpreted as a way of getting a skill that they possessed recognised as important, and thereby to bring themselves closer to power, displacing those who held it up to then. This was particularly true for the linguistic minorities in the Austro-Hungarian Empire, who were hoping to acquire power for their local language groups at the expense of the German-speaking imperial authorities.

The right-wing nationalism of the end of the nineteenth century, which went on to grow into the fascist movements of the inter-war period, was a means for those outside power to attempt to regain it. The old right who had lost power with the coming of the nation-state and increased democracy attempted through nationalist appeals to regain the influence they had lost. Nationalism can therefore be seen as a reactive ideology, adopted in self-defence in the face of humiliation or relative weakness in order to change society in a way that will benefit the nationalistic group.

Because of its roots in the social and political balance between the weak and the strong both within and between states, it would seem that nationalism must always lead to the kind of conflicts which have been examined throughout this book. Conflict does not necessarily imply violence, however, and certainly need not do so to the extent realised in the mass wars and racial genocide of the first half of the twentieth century. Where there has been extreme humiliation or exclusion from power, conflicts arising out of nationalism, steeped in powerful imagery and rhetoric, are perhaps particularly susceptible to leading to violence, as they did in Europe between 1789 and 1945. It is however possible for nationalist political conflicts to be resolved in non-violent ways.

Democracy and the nation

One final theme which has been hinted at, but not yet clearly stated, is the link between the ideology of the nation as sovereign and democracy. The historical association is a close one, for during the French Revolution the legal concept of the sovereignty of the nation – meaning the people – implied that power should not be hereditary, but in the hands of the whole population. Not all self-confessing nationalists throughout the history of nationalism have believed in universal suffrage, but most have had at least some awareness that democracy and the idea of limiting absolute power through elections were worthwhile principles. Ultimately, those principles implied universal suffrage, and the history of the rise of nations is in some ways also the history of the rise of democracy and its progress towards universal suffrage.

Since some common base is necessary for democracy to work, the desire to have the population participate in national affairs through democracy implied that the people needed to be educated. Because a sense of national solidarity and belonging is not a natural, inbuilt one, the combination of democracy and the division of territory into sovereign nations encouraged all nations at some point in their history to embark on a project of cultural assimilation through the education of their people. Cultural homogeneity and the thorough penetration and acceptance of the national identity on the part of the whole population was indeed the only way of ensuring that the newly established national order would retain its control, and of guaranteeing the territorial integrity of the nation. In its absence some of the people might decide that they were part of a different nation, or that a smaller region constituted not a part of the greater nation, but a nation on its own with the right to independence. Cultural assimilation by inventing an image of the nation, and then convincing the people that they were an integral part of it, was an effective method of securing their loyalty. In addition, a homogeneous population permitted the nation-states to control their national economies more tightly and to regulate society through their administration more effectively and thoroughly.

Once the victory of the national forces over absolutism was secure, therefore, most of the European nation-states we have examined sought to educate their population in such a way as to assimilate their people and extend the franchise to a greater number of voters. One of the dangers of cultural assimilation, and of basing national identity on homogeneity, is the tendency to use racial terms. This can lead to exclusiveness, which is dangerous when carried to an extreme – as happened in Germany in the 1930s and early 1940s. This is not an inevitable consequence of nationalism, however, for it is also possible, among the many combinations of characteristics which can contribute to national identities, to select models that are less racist and less intent upon rivalry, and that include elements of tolerance. Examples of multi-ethnic nations do exist, such as Switzerland; as do examples of nations which constitute what is effectively a cultural mosaic, in which different communities or regions are permitted to retain local cultural institutions and elements of cultural distinctiveness – such as Flanders in Belgium and Catalonia in Spain.

At the end of this study, which has followed the development of nationalism from its origins through the terrible conflicts it has provoked, it is worth pointing out that one of the biggest challenges that our modern democratic nation-states have yet to meet is the attempt to combine national unity with cultural tolerance.

Select bibliography

Much has been written about nationalism, both the theory behind it and its practical consequences in history. Most general textbooks about nineteenth-century Europe will have a chapter or a section devoted to its study, and discussions of it appear in many other works of history. What follows is a brief overview of some of the most important books for those who wish to begin further investigation of the subject.

The theory of nationalism

There is a wide variety of work dealing with the nature of nationalism and its causes, in an attempt to seek a pattern and to try to understand the features common to all nationalisms. Some of the most useful include P. Alter, *Nationalism*, London, 1989; B. Anderson, *Imagined communities. Reflections on the origin and spread of nationalism*, London, 1986; J. A. Armstrong, *Nations before nationalism*, Chapel Hill, NC, 1982; J. Breuilly, *Nationalism and the state*, 2nd edn, Manchester, 1993; E. Gellner, *Nations and nationalism*, Oxford, 1983; E. J. Hobsbawm, *Nations and nationalism since 1780: programme, myth, reality*, 2nd edn, Cambridge, 1992; E. J. Hobsbawm and T. Ranger (eds.), *The invention of tradition*, Cambridge, 1983; J. Hutchinson and A. D. Smith (eds.), *Nationalism*, Oxford, 1994; J. Krejci and V. Velimsky, *Ethnic and political nations in Europe*, London, 1981; A. D. Smith, *Theories of nationalism*, London, 1983.

See A. Hastings, *The construction of nationhood: ethnicity, religion and nationalism*, Cambridge, 1997, for a criticism of the views of Anderson, Hobsbawm and Gellner.

For a collection of primary documents, see S. Woolf (ed.), *Nationalism in Europe 1815 to the present: a reader*, London, 1996.

Individual countries

For a development of nationalism in a specific country or region, see D. G. Boyce, *Nationalism in Ireland*, London, 1982; J. F. Bradley, *Czech nationalism in the nineteenth century*, Boulder, Col., 1984; R. Brubaker, *Citizenship and nationhood in France and Germany*, Cambridge, Mass., 1992; R. Colls and P. Dodd (eds.), *Englishness, politics and culture 1880–1920*, London, 1986; M. Hroch, *Social preconditions of national revival in Europe. A comparative analysis of the social composition of patriotic groups among the smaller European nations*, Cambridge, 1985; B. Jenkins, *Nationalism in France: class and nation since 1789*, London, 1990; R. F. Leslie (ed.), *The history of Poland since 1863*, Cambridge, 1980; E. Niederhauser, *The rise of nationality in eastern Europe*, Budapest, 1982; H. Schulze (ed.), *Nation-building in central Europe*, Leamington Spa, 1987; and L. L. Snyder, *Roots of German nationalism*, Bloomington, 1978.

M. Teich and R. Porter (eds.), *The national question in Europe in historical context*, Cambridge, 1993, contains articles on several of the European nations.

Chronology

Chronology

1861	Unification of Italy; Cavour gives it a constitution
1866	*3 July:* Victory of Prussia over Austria at Sadowa followed by formation of Confederation of Northern Germany around Prussia
1867	Universal male suffrage introduced in German Confederation
	December: Hungary given separate parliament
1870	Gladstone adopts Elementary Education Act in Great Britain
	1 September: Victory of Prussia over France at Sedan
	20 September: Italian troops enter Rome, which becomes capital of kingdom of Italy on 1 August 1871
1871	*18 January:* William II proclaimed emperor of newly united Germany
1872	Beginning of *Kulturkampf* in Germany
	Publication of *The possessed* by Fyodor Dostoevsky
	24 June: Disraeli's speech at Crystal Palace
	13–26 August: First performance of Wagner's *Ring cycle* at Bayreuth
1877	Queen Victoria proclaimed empress of India
1885	*28 July:* Jules Ferry's speech in French Chamber of Deputies
1890	Bismarck's fall from power
1891	*9 April:* Creation of Pan-German League favourable to ideas of *Mittel Europa* and of division of world into zones of influence
1896	*18 January:* William II announces *Weltpolitik*
1897	Publication of *Les Déracinés* by Barrès
1898	Dreyfus Affair in France
1899	Foundation of *Action Française* by Charles Maurras
1902	Publication of *Imperialism: a study* by J. A. Hobson
1903	*November:* Creation of review *The kingdom* by Corradini
1910	*3 December:* Foundation of Italian Nationalist Association, with Corradini's participation
1912	Universal male suffrage in Italy
1914	*August:* First World War begins
	December: Home Rule Bill for Ireland passed by British parliament (operation suspended until end of war)
1917	*October:* Bolshevik revolution in Russia
1918	*8 January:* Woodrow Wilson's Fourteen Points
	11 November: Armistice ends First World War
1919	*January:* Spartacist uprising in Germany
	February: Creation of League of Nations
	28 June: Treaty of Versailles – Europe tentatively rebuilt according to the principle of nationality
1920	Government of Ireland Act
1922	*24 October:* Mussolini's Naples speech
	30 October: Mussolini gains power in Italy
	6 December: Irish Free State established by royal proclamation

1924 Hitler writes *Mein Kampf*

1925 *October:* Locarno pact

1926 Germany joins League of Nations

1928 *27 August:* Kellogg–Briand pact

1929 Wall Street stock market crash – Great Depression starts

1933 *30 January:* Hitler becomes chancellor in Germany
October: Germany withdraws from League of Nations
15 November: Goebbels' speech 'The new tasks of German culture'

1936 *7 March:* German troops reoccupy Rhineland – Treaty of Locarno destroyed
17 July: Beginning of civil war in Spain

1938 *12 March: Anschluss* of Austria to Third Reich
29 September: Munich accord

1939 *March:* Victory of Franco's nationalist forces in Spain
1 September: Invasion of Poland by Germany
3 September: Britain and France declare war on Germany
26 September: Poland capitulates

1940 *22 June:* France signs armistice with Germany

1942 *20 January:* Decision in Germany to adopt Final Solution to Jewish question –
beginning of Holocaust

1945 *February:* Yalta conference – division of world into two ideologically opposed blocs;
national question seems to fall into background

Index

Index

Romanticism, 15–16, 21–3, 40; and the
Enlightenment, 15; and Italian unification,
18; and national literature and music,
15–16, 85
Rousseau, Jean-Jacques, 5
Russia, 14, 52; and German unification, 19;
and Empire, 53, 56; and Napoleon, 79–80;
and the Polish insurrection (1839), 16;
revolution (1917), 72, 76; and the Soviet
Union, 79–80

Saint-Just, Louis Antoine, 43
Schönerer, Georg, 54
Scotland, 86
Second World War, 79–80
secret societies, 16, 18; Young Germany, 16;
Young Ireland, 16; Young Italy, 16, 18
Serbia, 36; border settlement (1919), 73, 81
Sieyès, abbé Emmanuel Joseph, 6, 9
sovereignty, *see* legitimacy
Spain, 15–16, 29, 89; and fascism, 77; and
imperialism, 66
Spanish Civil War, 77
Soviet Union: and the post-war period, 86;
and the Second World War, 79–80; and the
Spanish Civil War, 77
Stein, Karl von, 13
Stresemann, Gustav, 75–6
Switzerland, 3, 26, 31, 59, 89

Third Estate, 6, 9, 87

Ukraine, 52
United States: and the League of Nations, 75;
and the post-war period, 86

Valmy, battle of (1792), 7
Versailles, treaty of (1919), 72–3, 75
Victor-Emmanuel II, king of Italy, 18
Victoria, queen of Great Britain, 63
Vienna, treaty of (1815), 12–13, 62

Wagner, Richard, 54–5
Weber, Max, 57, 58–60
William I, emperor of Germany, 19
William II, emperor of Germany, and
Weltpolitik, 66
Wilson, Woodrow, President of the United
States, 72–3, 75, 81–2
working class: composition, 45; and the First
World War, 71; and the French Revolution,
43; and internationalism, 45–6, 50, 59; and
Marxism, 44–50, 59

Yugoslavia, creation of (1919), 73

Zollverein, 19